The World as Image

Other books from the same Author

1. **Dharma, The Categorial Imperative**; edited by Ashok Vohara, Arvind Sharma and Mrinal Miri; ISBN 81-246-0270-0
2. **A New Curve in the Ganges** — Mahatma Gandhi's Interpretation of Hinduism; by Arvind Sharma; ISBN 81-246-0271-9
3. **New Focus on Hindu Studies**; by Arvind Sharma; ISBN 81-246-0307-3
4. **Sea-shell as Silver** — A Metaphorial Excursion into Advaita Vedānta; by Arvind Sharma; ISBN 81-246-0352-9
5. **The World as Dream**; by Arvind Sharma; ISBN 81-246-0365-0

The World as Image

Arvind Sharma
McGill University

D.K. Printworld (P) Ltd.
New Delhi

Cataloging in Publication Data — DK
[Courtesy: D.K. Agencies (P) Ltd. <docinfo@dkagencies.com>]

Sharma, Arvind, 1940–
The world as image / Arvind Sharma.
vii, 110 p. 23 cm.
Includes bibliographical references (p.)
Includes indexes.
ISBN 8124603626

1. Metaphor — Religious aspects — Hinduism.
2. Advaita. 3. Philosophy, Hindu. I. Title.

DDC 181.4 22

ISBN 81-246-0362-6
First published in India in 2006

Published and printed by:
D.K. Printworld (P) Ltd.
Regd. Office: 'Sri Kunj', F-52, Bali Nagar
New Delhi-110 015
Phones: (011) 2545-3975; 2546-6019; *Fax*: (011) 2546-5926
E-mail: dkprintworld@vsnl.net
Website: www.dkprintworld.com

Preface

HUMAN beings are remarkable creatures; they not only want to know the unknown, they also want to know the unknowable. They want to be present at the birth of their grandmother. This is how some philosophers would like to characterise their desire to know how the world came to be, although they themselves were born in the world after it had come into existence.

Be that as it may, the desire to know the unknowable in some cases is hard to fault. The ultimate reality in Advaita Vedānta, referred to as *Brahman*, is considered unknowable in the conventional sense of the term. It is also considered to be the sole spiritual reality which paradoxically accounts for the multiplicity of perceived objects and perceiving subjects in the universe. How is this possible?

Advaita Vedānta resorts to several analogies and images to render such a juxtaposition credible. One such approach resorts to the phenomenon of an image — like our reflection in a mirror — to do so. This book is an exploration of its many-splendoured use in Advaita Vedānta.

Contents

1

Introduction

THE step-mother of Snow White could look at the mirror and exclaim:

> Mirror, mirror on the wall
> Who's the fairest of them all

One supposes she wanted the mirror to reflect the truth but not to be too impartial in its judgement.

Reflections have long intrigued humanity, on account of the ambiguous relationship of the reflection to the original object of reflection. The relationship is so ambiguous as to be mysterious and so mysterious as to arouse wonder. It has even been so wondrous as to suggest a supernatural dimension, ranging from the prophetic to the metaphysical.

Thus the Master could instruct his disciple regarding the ultimacy of pure consciousness in these words:

> 51. The universe is, always and all-through, a phenomenon in the Self. The question then arises how consciousness, being void, is dense at the same time.
>
> 52. Just as a mirror, though dense and impenetrable, contains the image, so also pure consciousness is dense and impenetrable and yet displays the universe by virtue of its self-sufficiency.

> 53. Though consciousness is all-pervading, dense and single, it still holds the mobile and immobile creation within it, wonderful in its variety, with no immediate or ultimate cause for it.
>
> 54-55. Just as the mirror remains unaffected by the passage of different images and yet continues to reflect as clearly as before, so also the one consciousness illumines the waking and dream states which can be verified by proper meditation.[1]

Again the reflection can both attract or repel, strangely enough, depending on the features of the onlooker! Narcissus thought himself so beautiful he fell in love with himself, and wasted away, a warning perhaps against taking oneself too seriously. Narcissus had one kind of fate in store for him. However "tiger, tiger burning bright" met with a different fate. The tiger leapt at its own image as reflected in the still pond, dived at it, and has not been heard from since. Narcissus, the youth, fell in love with his own reflection in the water; the tiger fell into it. Strange pitfalls, once we reflect on them.

Small wonder then that the metaphor of reflection came to play a significant role as the mind of human beings tried to delve into the mystery of their being, and of their existence in the world. In fact, in Chinese thought, the mind itself was at times understood on the analogy of the mirror. Professor Weiming Tu once, in the course of a felicitous conversation, singled out three properties of the mirror which the mind shares with it and at which the Chinese marvelled. These were (1) receptivity, (2) purity and (3) transparency. A mirror can reflect anything just as the mind can think of anything. The mirror

---

1. Swami Sri Ramanananda Saraswathi, tr., *Tripura Rahasya* or *The Mystery Beyond the Trinity*, Tiruvannamalai: Sri Ramanasramam, 1980, p. 105.

always remained pure, irrespective of the quality of the object reflected in it. The mirror could reflect dirt without being dirtied by it, for instance. And the mirror is transparent in the sense that one can see through the space covered by its surface onto the objects reflected. So also one could transparently see the contents of the human mind through reflection. To these we may also add autonomy: the independence of the mirror from the objects reflected in the mirror. This Chinese disposition to compare the mind with the mirror, or *vice versa*, may have provided a common background which Buddhism could share when it moved into China. One does not find many examples of the use of the imagery of reflection in early Buddhism, but, already, in the earliest phase of Mahāyāna Buddhism the metaphor of reflection begins to come into its own. With the spread of Mahāyāna Buddhism, the metaphor of reflection became more popular. The *Laṅkāvatāra-Sūtra* declares:

> 159. In a mirror, in water, in an eye, in a vessel, and in gems, images can be seen. But the images in turn do not come from anywhere real.
>
> 160. A mere appearance of existence is thus the variety of things, like a mirage in the air. It is seen in a variety of forms, like a barren woman's child in a dream.[2]

In trying to explicate these ethereal pictures of what things are like, Asaṅga, with the help of some of Vasubandhu's comments, explains *Mahāyānasaṁgraha* II.27 with the help of ten metaphors. Three of these — of an image, a reflection and "moon reflected in water" are relevant here.

---

2. Edward Conze, et al, eds., *Buddhist Texts Through the Ages*, New York: Harper & Row, 1964, p. 215.

> 4. One may ask, "How, in the absence of an object, can wholesome and unwholesome actions produce desirable or undesirable fruits?" In answer, things are compared to an image — The image is not the real object. It is relative to a model that one produces the notion of an image. Yet, as distinct from the model, it has no reality. Likewise a desirable or undesirable fruit, though unreal, can be perceived.
>
> 5. One may ask, "How, in the absence of objects, can different acts of consciousness arise?" In answer, things are compared to a reflection — In a shadow play one sees all sorts of things reflected. Although these reflections are seen they are not really what they seem to be. In the same way, acts of consciousness are not different things, although they appear to be so.
>
> 7. One may ask, "How, in the absence of an object, can the images apperceived in trance arise?" In answer, things are compared to the moon reflected in water — The moon reflected in water is not really in the water, and yet, because the water is wet and limpid, the moon is seen in it. So with concentrated thought. The objects which form its range are not real things, and yet they are perceived, the state of trance playing the part of water.[3]

When Buddhism entered China it sometimes took recourse to the metaphor of reflection to make its point. For instance, one Master of the Hua-yen school, which bases itself on the *Avataṁsaka* or the Garland Sūtra, employed the metaphor quite literally to illustrate its basic principle of: "one in all and all in one," which blends its "two fundamental principles, that the absolute and phenomenon are interfused

---

3. *Ibid.*, pp. 215-216. For a critical analysis of Vasubandhu's views see Chakravarthi Ram-Prasad, *Advaita Epistemology and Metaphysics: An Outline of Indian Non-Realism*, London: Routledge Curzon, 2002, Chapter 2.

with each other, and that all phenomena are mutually related one with another."[4]

This concept of the mutual interpenetration and even identification of the *dharma*s comes to vivid life when illustrated with the help of reflection. Fa-tsang, the master of the Hua-yen school, first employed a different metaphor. He tried to illustrate the point with the image of a lion made of gold. If the entire lion is made of gold then each organ can be said to be related to all other organs by virtue of them all sharing the property of being cast in the same gold. Each of the lion's organs is present in the whole lion. This point is easier to grasp than the next, that the entire golden lion is also present in a part, even in a single strand of hair. It is recorded in the fifth chapter of the text Sung Kao-seng-chuan that when the students failed to grasp this point, Fa-tsang resorted to the following experiment:

> He prepared ten mirrors, with eight placed at the eight points of the compass, one above, and one below, all facing one another. In the center was placed the Buddha figure, lighted by a huge torch. The disciples now saw that not only was the image reflected in the mirrors but the image in each mirror was also reflected in all the other mirrors. Not only this, but the multiple images reflected in each were also reflected in every other mirror, thus doubling the redoubling of the images. This was like Indra's net, with its network of jewels that not only reflected the images in every other jewel, but also the multiple images in the others.[5]

---

4. Kenneth K.S. Ch'en, *Buddhism: The Light of Asia*, Woodbury, New York: Barron's Educational Series, Inc. 1968, p. 163.
5. Kenneth K.S. Ch'en, *Buddhism in China: A Historical Survey*, Princeton, New Jersey: Princeton University Press, 1964, p. 317.

The use of the metaphor of reflection is perhaps equally, if not even more, celebrated in the Ch'an tradition of Buddhism in China. Some have even interpreted the celebrated wall-gazing of Bodhidharma (*circa* sixth century) in terms of the metaphor of reflection, or rather in terms of the absence of reflection. When a would-be disciple, Wu, approached him Bodhidharma was sitting facing the wall. Wu asked him, "Why are you facing the wall? Why do you not see me? Why do you not see others?" Bodhidharma said, "For my whole life I was facing you and all others, but in their eyes I never saw anything other than a dead wall, so I decided that it is better to face the wall. One is at ease, as one knows that there is a wall. But when facing someone and feeling the wall there, it becomes difficult. I can talk with you more easily because you are behind and I am not seeing you."[6]

By the time of the Sixth Patriarch, Hui-neng, when Ch'an Buddhism had become firmly established in China, the metaphor of reflection came to play a role in the selection of the Patriarch itself, and not merely in "patriarchal" meditation and realization. The story of the succession of Hui-neng as the Sixth Patriarch is fairly well-known but bears retelling on account of the decisive centrality of the metaphor of reflection in the episode. "One day the Fifth Patriarch [Hung-jen] suddenly called all his pupils to come to him. As they assembled, he said:

> Let me say this to you. Birth and death are serious matters. You people are engaged all day in making offerings [to the Buddha], going after blessings and rewards only, and you make no effort to achieve freedom from the bitter sea of life and death. Your self-nature seems to be obscured. How can blessings save

---

6. Bhagwan Shree Rajneesh, *I Am the Gate*, Bombay: A Life Awakening Movement Publication, 1972, p. 206.

you? Go to your rooms and examine yourselves. He who is enlightened use his perfect vision of self-nature and write me a verse. When I look at his verse, if it reveals deep understanding, I shall give him the robe and the Law and make him the Sixth Patriarch. Hurry, hurry!

At midnight Shen-hsiu, holding a candle, wrote a verse on the wall of the south corridor, without anyone knowing about it, which said:

> Our body is the tree of Perfect Wisdom,
> And our mind is a bright mirror.
> At all times diligently wipe them,
> So that they will be free from dust. [Sec. 6]

The Fifth Patriarch said: The verse you wrote shows some but not all understanding. You have arrived at the front of the door but you have not yet entered it. Ordinary people, by practising in accordance with your verse, will not degenerate. But it will be futile to seek the Supreme Perfect Wisdom while holding to such a view. One must enter the door and see his self-nature. Go away and come back after one or two days of thought. If you have entered the door and seen your self-nature, I shall give you the robe and the Law.

Shen-hsiu went away and for several days could not produce another verse.

Hui-neng also wrote a verse . . . which says:

> The tree of Perfect Wisdom is originally no tree.
> Nor has the bright mirror any frame.
> Buddha-nature is forever clear and pure.
> Where is there any dust?

Another verse:

> The mind is the tree of Perfect Wisdom.
> The body is the clear mirror.
> The clear mirror is originally clear and pure.
> Where has it been affected by any dust?

> Monks in the hall were all surprised at these verses. Hui-neng, however, went back to the rice-pounding room. The Fifth Patriarch suddenly realized that Hui-neng was the one of good knowledge but was afraid lest the rest learn it. He therefore told them: "This will not do."
>
> The Fifth Patriarch waited till midnight, called Hui-neng to come to the hall, and expounded the Diamond Sūtra. As soon as Hui-neng heard this, he understood. That night the Law was imparted to him without anyone knowing it, and thus the Law and the robe [emblematic] of Sudden Enlightenment were transmitted to him. "You are now the Sixth Patriarch," said the Fifth Patriarch to Hui-neng, "The robe is the testimony of transmission from generation to generation. As to the Law, it is to be transmitted from mind to mind. Let people achieve understanding through their own effort."
>
> The Fifth Patriarch told Hui-neng: "From the very beginning, the transmission of the Law has been as delicate as a hanging thread of silk. If you remain here, someone might harm you. You had better leave quickly." [Sec. 9][7]

The metaphor of reflection came to be widely employed in Japan as well. The Vijñānavādins in "the course of their long history of speculations on the different types of wisdom arrived at a definite scheme regarding them. According to this scheme four kinds of wisdom are visualized (*catvāri jñānāni*). They are *ādarśa-jñāna, samatā-jñāna, pratyavekṣaṇā-jñāna* and *kṛtyanuṣṭhāna-jñāna*."[8] "Kukai in his Hizoki gives an interesting illustration of these forms of wisdom using the

7. Wm. Theodore de Bary et al, eds., *Sources of Chinese Tradition*, New York: Columbia University Press, 1960, Volume I. pp. 350-51.

8. S. Kanoaka, "Ādarśa-Jñāna" in G.P. Malalasekara, ed., *Encyclopaedia of Buddhism*, Government of Ceylon (Sri Lanka), 1961, vol I, p. 189.

metaphor of water as follows: The clear surface of water can represent everything in the same way as could a mirror. This will correspond to *ādarśa-jñana*. The figures of everything reflected on the surface of water are completely equal without a higher or a lower. This will correspond to *samatā-jñāna*."[9]

In Japan, however, the metaphor moved from the realm of religion to culture. If we accept Paul Tillich's statement that "religion is the substance of culture and culture the form of religion,"[10] then we might say that the metaphor had begun to extend itself beyond substance to form. Japanese culture is distinguished by both a martial and a natural tradition: the cultivation of the virtue of a warrior as a fine art (*Bushido*) and a devotion to the simple beauty of nature are celebrated in numerous ways. The metaphor of reflection can be identified in both these aspects of Japanese culture. The final certificate awarded in the Shinkage-ryu, "one of the most popular schools of swordsmanship in the feudal days of Japan"[11] consisted of:

> nothing but a circle. This is supposed to represent a mirror bright and altogether free from film and dust, and its meaning is no doubt the allusion to the Buddhist epistemology of the "great-perfect-mirror-wisdom," which is no other than the Prajñā Immovable. . . . The swordsman's mind must be kept entirely free from selfish affects and intellectual calculations so the "original intuition" is ready to work at its best —

9. *Ibid*.

10. Quoted in Troy Wilson Organ, *Hinduism: Its Historical Development*, Woodbury, New York: Barron's Educational Series, Inc., 1974, p. 10.

11. Daisetz T. Suzuki, *Zen and Japanese Culture*, New York: Pantheon Books, 1959, p. 121.

> which is a state of no-mind-ness. Mere technical skill in the use of the sword does not necessarily give one full qualification as a swordsmaster. He must Realize the final state of spiritual discipline, which is to attain no-mind-ness, symbolized as a circle empty of contents — a circle with no circumference.[12]

The second of the five key points which elucidate Yagyu Shinkage's position on the relationship between Zen and swordsmanship, cited below, seems to require no further comment as it confirms and conforms to the point under discussion:

> The second topic is concerned with the "base" or "seat" which the swordsman is to occupy. It is entitled "the moon and water." It is taken from one of the Buddhist similes that are used to illustrate the quickness or immediacy with which the mind perceives an object appearing before it. When the moon reveals itself behind a mass of clouds, as they are dispersed, it is reflected immediately on the water. It is the same with the mirror that reflects the flower as soon as the latter presents itself before it. So with the swordsman's position or base when he stands before his opponent, it must be such that he can readily invade the latter's field at his own pleasure and with the immediacy of the moon reflecting itself on the water.[13]

The simultaneous proximity to Nature and Reality, as intuited in Zen, can also be brought home through the metaphor of reflection, as when one is told:

> Let us destroy all such artificial barriers we put up between Nature and ourselves, for it is only when they are removed that we see into the living heart of Nature and live with it —

---

12. *Ibid*.
13. *Ibid*. p. 162.

> which is the real meaning of love. For this, therefore, the clearing away of all conceptual scaffolds is imperative. When Zen speaks of transparency, it means this clearing away, this thorough wiping of the surface of the mind-mirror. But, in point of fact, the mirror has never been obscured, and no need has ever been felt for wiping it clean; but because of such notions as identity, tranquility, one spirit, egotistic commotions, and so on, we are compelled to set up a general sweeping operation.[14]

In fact, in later developments when the conversation between a Master and a disciple is encountered, sometimes one would not know whether the passage was of Hindu or Buddhist until the context was provided. Consider, for instance, the following:

> Student: I feel myself a prisoner of my ego and want to escape. . .
>
> Master: Let us speak of mind first. Your mind can be compared to a mirror, which reflects everything that appears before it. From the time you begin to think, to feel, and to exert your will, shadows are cast upon your mind which distort its reflections. This condition we call delusion, which is the fundamental sickness in that it creates a sense of duality, in consequence of which you postulate "I" and "not-I." The truth is that everything is One, and this of course is not a numerical One. Falsely seeing oneself confronted by a world of separate existence, this is what creates antagonism, greed, and, inevitable suffering.[15]

This passage is not a passage from an ancient text of Advaita Vedānta. It is presented from a contemporary Zen manual in a mildly modified form.

---

14. *Ibid.*, p. 351.
15. Philip Kapleau, ed., *The Three Pillars of Zen*, New York: Harper & Row, 1966, p. 96.

One could pursue the theme of the metaphor of the world as an image in a particular culture — Chinese, Indian, Japanese, for instance, or in a particular religion — Taoism, Hinduism, Buddhism given its universality. This universality of the metaphor was documented in this chapter. One may now focus on its deployment within a particular school of Hindu philosophy, such as that of Advaita Vedānta.

2

The Metaphor of Reflection in Advaita Vedānta

ONE of the basic tenets of Advaita Vedānta may be worth emphasizing by way of transition, namely, that there is ultimately only *one* reality. Advaita Vedānta is so firmly committed to this position that it is even coy about describing it as monism — it calls it non-dualism to prevent the postulation of any duality prior to this unity. This doctrine is obviously in apparent conflict with our normal experience of life, which is characterized by multiplicity. Much intellectual effort has been expended in Advaita Vedānta to establish the plausibility of its apparently astonishing claim that the experience of multiplicity is metaphysically false. The metaphor of the world as image is often invoked in this context. It is to a consideration of these issues that we now turn.

A key philosophical issue thus lies embedded at the very core of Advaita Vedānta: if the ultimate reality is non-dual, how do we explain the apparent plurality of the world, especially the apparent plurality of living beings or *jīva*s?

Although the issue of how any entity presumed to be unitary becomes a plurality is potentially a philosophically vexatious issue, it is especially so when that entity is considered spiritual and not material in nature.[1] It is easier to explain how pots, cups and saucers of different sizes may emerge from the same clay, than to explain how the one undifferentiated consciousness could be visualized as functioning in several different loci of consciousness called *jīvas*.

It was the attempt to answer this question satisfactorily which made Advaitins resort to the metaphor of reflection. Among the early Advaitins it remained just that — a metaphor, but it soon developed into the hands of post-Śaṅkaran

---

1. Prima facie there is no reason why the one ultimate reality may not be material as suggested by the materialists (see M. Hiriyanna, *The Essentials of Indian Philosophy,* [London: George Allen & Unwin, 1948] p. 59 and *The Outlines of Indian Philosophy,* [London: George Allen & Unwin, 1932] p. 192). Śaṅkara is clearly aware of both the possibilities but opts for the spiritual option on the following grounds. "Śaṅkara contends that the cause of the world cannot be mere unconscious matter, because the *Brahman* must be the sole cause of the world, that is, both the efficient and the material. As no efficient cause can be insensient or *jaḍa*, the *Brahman* must be conscious. Śaṅkara does not advance the argument that matter which is insensient cannot produce mind which is consciousness. He says that, in the world, we see that from the sensient human body, insensient things, like hair and nails, are born and from insensient rotten matter, like cow-dung, etc. insects and worms, which are sensient, are born. But he tells us that pure matter by itself cannot plan out creation, and so needs the help of consciousness. Nor can we say that the cause of the world is two-fold, both matter and consciousness. The *Brahman* alone must be the cause, as otherwise matter may not conform to its activity. Therefore we have to admit that it is conscious. This is the basic argument of Śaṅkara against the Sāṅkhya theory of Prakṛti." (P.T. Raju, *Idealist Thought of India* [London: George Allen & Unwin, 1952] p. 122.

Advaitins from a metaphor into a metaphysical position and it was reified into what has been called the theory of "reflexionism."[2]

Among the earliest Advaitins, if we are to count Aṣṭāvakra as one,[3] the issue was phrased somewhat differently. Its poetic statement may have prevented it from being perceived as a philosophical problem. Verses 23-25 of Chapter II of *Aṣṭāvakra Gītā* illustrate the point:

> 23. O, in the boundless ocean of myself as the winds of mind arise, manifold worlds quickly appear as its waves.
>
> 24. In the infinite ocean of myself as the winds of mind are stilled, the creature-merchant finds its world-vessel transitory due to the vicissitudes of life.
>
> 25. It is a marvel that in the boundless ocean of myself creatures like waves rise, jostle, play with one another and merge spontaneously.[4]

In the last verse the expression *jīvavīcaya* occurs, thereby removing any doubt that the issue of the multiplicity of *jīva*s is involved.

The emphasis at this stage of Advaita seems to have on establishing the essential non-difference of *jīva* from Brahman, rather than in seeking an explanation of its origin, or developing models thereof in the first place. Therefore although "the teachers of Advaita *after* Śaṅkara have differed among themselves over the mode in which the non-difference

---

2. Eliot Deutsch and J.A.B. van Buitenen, *A Source Book of Advaita Vedānta*, Honolulu: The University Press of Hawaii, 1971, p. 242.
3. Radhakamal Mukherjee, *The Song of the Self Supreme* (*Aṣṭāvakragītā*), Delhi: Motilal Banarsidass, 1971, p. 5.
4. *Ibid.*, pp. 49-50.

is to be explained,"[5] and have in the main been advocates of what are known as *pratibimbavāda* (reflection-theory) or *avaccedavāda* (limitation-theory), those Advaitins such as Guaḍapāda who *preceded* Śaṅkara should not be uncritically aligned with these positions. For instance, "illustration of ether is worked out in detail by Guaḍapāda.[6] But on that account it is not right to say that he preferred the *avaccheda* view to the *pratibimbavāda*. Such a problem did not arise in his time. He employs the term "ābhāsa," too which means reflection or appearance. All that he is intent on teaching is that, shorn of the adjuncts, the *jīva* is non-different from Brahman."[7]

Reflection analogies are employed by Śaṅkara to explain how the One could become many, as well as to explain *both* how a transcendental One could be consistent with a plurality of subjects *and* a multiplicity of objects. Karl H. Potter remarks:

> These are probably the most complex and sophisticated of the models offered by Śaṅkara and his contemporaries. They are invoked by Śaṅkara to explain the relation between God and the *jīva*s. Śaṅkara says that the *jīva*s are mere "appearances" or "reflections" (*ābhāsa*) of the Highest Self, as when the sun is reflected in rippling water. The analogy is used to rebut an argument by an opponent who wonders why, if there is only one Self operating the various bodies, the actions of the various bodies do not get mixed up. Śaṅkara's answer is that when the sun is reflected in several *ābhāsa*s the trembling of one such reflection does not require that the next one also tremble; no more so in the case of one individual self's actions — they need not affect the next self.

---

5. T.M.P. Mahadevan, *Gauḍapāda: A Study in Early Advaita,* University of Madras (Chennai), 1960, p. 163, emphasis added.
6. *Ibid.*, pp. 164-69.
7. *Ibid.*, p. 164.

> Śaṅkara also invokes the reflection analogy to explain how qualityless *Brahman*, consciousness only, can appear as many objects in our experience. In *Brahmasūtrabhāṣya* III.2.11 21 an objector points out that in the case of the sun there is something different from the sun, namely, rippling water, for the sun to be reflected in, whereas there is nothing different from *Brahman*. Śaṅkara admits that this is a dissimilarity — no analogy is perfect — but argues that there are a number of points of similarity nevertheless. For example, Brahman, like the sun, appears to be affected when the nature of the reflecting medium changes — when, for example, it becomes dirty and the light becomes pallid — but neither Brahman nor the sun are really affected.[8]

The problem of the reflecting medium is here to stay. In a way it is helpful for it lets things happen to the reflection while at the same time the source of reflection remains untouched. It also helps Śaṅkara philosophically explain a mythical account of creation:

> Śaṅkara uses reflection to explain the Upaniṣadic passage that says that the Self enters into the universe. Of course the Self, being nondifferent from the universe, cannot literally enter it, but it enters it just as the sun "enters" the water by being perceived there in its reflection, though of course it doesn't literally enter the water. This use of the analogy implies that the undifferentiated universe, like Sāṁkhya's *avyakta prakṛti,* is the medium that reflects pure consciousness, *Brahman,* with the *jīva*s perceiving the Self and themselves in that medium in varied ways.[9]

---

8. Karl H. Potter, ed., *Encyclopedia of Indian Philosophies,* Delhi: Motilal Banarsidass, 1981, Volume III, pp. 84-85.

9. *Ibid.,* p. 85.

But its greatest advantage still lies in the fact that the different fates of the *jīvas*, and in fact the very fact of the apparently many different *jīvas*, a more crucial philosophical issue, can be handled with finesse. Yet the house is still haunted by the ghost of the reflecting medium.

Śaṅkara basically uses three strategies to exorcise the ghost, when its presence gets philosophically too poltergeistic. This result is achieved by resorting to other analogies which eliminate the medium. One of them is that of the red crystal. A piece of rock crystal sitting on the shelf may appear to be red in colour because there is a red flower behind it, not noticed by the observer. Although Śaṅkara appeals occasionally to this analogy, it is Maṇḍana Miśra who explains it most completely. "The advantage of this model is that it sheds light on the necessity of removing the medium so that the prototype — the crystal, or *Brahman* — may be directly seen, even though the form of the crystal was not entirely obliterated by the flower it reflected."[10] But far more common with Śaṅkara is the use of the analogy of ether, which removes the need of a reflecting medium. As he states in his commentary on the *Bṛhadāraṇyakopaniṣad*:

> The Supreme Self is intrinsically invisible, hence without parts; so a part of it cannot become the individual self. And if you say that the individual self is a part because of the imposition of some adjunct or obstruction, as the *ākāśa* enclosed in a jar is a part of the great *ākāśa*, then discriminating people would never think that the self is a part of the Self, since it would appear as something quite distinct. So any such notions about the self's difference from the Self are erroneous (*bhrānta*).[11]

---

10. *Ibid.*, p. 85.

11. *Ibid.*, p. 191.

In view of the fact that Śaṅkara uses both the reflection-theory and the limitation-theory, it seems promising to undertake a metaphorical comparison at this point to assess their use by Śaṅkara.

Three cases of the metaphor of reflection may be identified in the *Vivekacūḍāmaṇi*. One of them pertains to the *jīva*'s *relationship to the world* and is therefore not directly relevant here but is cited for the sake of completeness.

> 291. That in which there is this reflection of the universe, as of a city in a mirror — that *Brahman* art thou; knowing this thou wilt attain the consummation of thy life.[12]

The other one pertains to the *jīva's relationship to his own actions* and so is again not directly relevant but fills in the picture:

> 508. When the supervening adjunct* (*upādhi*) is moving, the resulting movement of the reflection is ascribed by fools to the object reflected, such as the sun, which is free from activity — (and they think) "I am** the doer," "I am the experiencer," "I am killed, oh, alas!"[13]

---

12. Swami Madhvananda, tr., *Vivekacūḍāmani of Śrī Śaṅkarācārya*, Calcutta (Kolkata): Advaita Ashrama, 1966, p. 114. For a more recent translation see John Grimes, *The Vivekacūḍāmaṇi of Śaṅkarācārya Bhagavatpāda: An Introduciotn and Translation*, Hants, England: Ashgate Publishing Company, 2004.
13. *Ibid.*, p. 195.

* Supervening adjunct — For example, water, in which the sun is reflected. It is the water that moves and with it the reflection, but not the sun, though ignorant people may think that it is also moving. Similarly, all activity which belongs to the intellect under the reflection of the *ātman*, is erroneously attributed to the latter.

** I am, etc. — This is how the ignorant man thinks and wails.

Interest now centres on the next two verses — one of which employs the reflection-theory and the other the limitation-theory. The movement from one to the other in quick succession is a striking movement from metaphorical richness to metaphysical austerity. The following two verses elaborate the metaphor of reflection:

> 218. Seeing the reflection of the sun mirrored in the water of a jar, the fool thinks it is the sun itself. Similarly the stupid man, through delusion, identifies himself with the reflection of the *cit** caught in the *buddhi,* which is Its superimposition.
>
> 219. Just as the wise man leaves aside the jar, the water and the reflection of the sun in it, and sees the self-luminous sun which illumines these three and is independent** of them; . . .[14]

Another verse in one sharp thrust however demonstrates the power of the limitation-theory:

> 565. As, when a jar is broken, the space enclosed by it becomes palpably the limitless space, so when the apparent limitations are destroyed, the knower of Brahman verily becomes *Brahman* Itself.[15]

The jar appears in both the metaphors — in one full of water, in the other empty. In one it is connected with the sun through the water; in the other with space through space. It is worth noting that the sun shines in space and is reflected in the *water* in the pot, not in the *space* in the pot, but through the space in the pot.

---

* *Cit* — The Atman which is Knowledge Absolute.]

** Independent, etc. — These being merely its reflections, which serve to suggest the real sun.].

14. *Ibid.*, p. 87.

15. *Ibid.*, p. 218.

T.M.P. Mahadevan remarks on the use of these two metaphors by Śaṅkara as follows: "The difference between the two views, *pratibimbavāda* and *avacchedavāda*, is the result of stretching the illustrations beyond their legitimate point. In Śaṅkara's writings both the illustrations are found. The point in the analogy of reflection as well as in that of pot-defined ether is that *jīvatva* is adventitious. There need be no discrepancy between regarding the *jīva* as a reflection and considering it to be nescience-defined intelligence."[16] While it may be true that there need be no discrepancy involved, it seems that a discrepancy could arise on account of the different metaphorical orientations involved and that it would be reflected in the understanding of the *mahāvākya*: *tat tvam asi*. Some have taken it as establishing the identity of *jīva* with Īśvara, while others have taken it to mean as asserting the identity of *ātman* and *Brahman*. If the grand dictum is understood within the framework of the reflection-theory it lends itself more naturally to the identification of *jīva* with Īśvara, as nescience has already entered the picture in a way it does not in the ethereal or spatial metaphor. The following remarks of Ramaṇa in this context become unexpectedly illuminating:

> This is exactly what is conveyed by the *Mahāvākya Tatvamasi* (You are That). Find yourself; and then "That" is known.
>
> D.: How is that Brahman?
>
> M.: Why do you want to know of *Brahman* apart from yourself? The scripture says "You are that." The Self is intimate to you and you cannot indeed be without the Self. Realise it. That is the Realisation of *Brahman* also.[17]

---

16. T.M.P. Mahadevan, *op. cit.*, p. 164.
17. *Talks with Śrī Ramaṇa Maharṣi*, Tiruvannamalai: Sri Ramanasramam, 1984, p. 284.

Elsewhere the *mahāvākya*: *tattvamsi* is again explained as follows:

> To reject the three bodies consisting of the five sheaths (physical, vital, mental, gnostic and delectant) as not "I" and to extract through subtle enquiry of "Who am I?" — even as the central blade of grass is delicately drawn out from its whorl — that which is different from all the three bodies and is existent as one and universal in the heart as Aham or "I" and denoted by the words Tvam (in the Scriptural dictum — *Tat-tvam-asi* — That thou art). This process of subtle enquiry is manana or deep contemplation.[18]

Another comment on the *mahāvākya* runs as follows:

> To a further question, M. answered: There are said to be *Pañcapada Mahāvākyani* (*mahāvākya*s with five words) e.g., *Tattvamasi atinijam* ("you are that" is the great truth). The first three words have their *lakṣya artha* (significance) all of which signify only the one Truth. So many efforts and so much discipline are said to be necessary for eradicating the non-existing avidyā![19]

Both of these previous remarks tie into the following explanation:

> Sri Bhagavan Ramaṇa said: Leaving out what is intimate and immediate, why should one seek the rest? The scriptures say "That Thou art." In this statement "Thou" is directly experienced; but leaving it out they go on seeking "That!"
>
> M.: "Thou" is the Inner Self immanent in all; in order to find the same, he leaves himself out and sees the world objectively. What is the world? What is Immanent in it? It is "That." All such ideas arise only on forgetting one's own Self. I never bothered myself with such matters. Only after a

18. *Ibid.*, p. 316.
19. *Ibid.*, p. 495.

> time it occurred to me that men had investigated such matters.[20]
>
> Some say that one must know the "tat" because the idea of the world constantly arises to deflect the mind. If the Reality behind it is first ascertained it will be found to be Brahman. The "*tvam*" is understood later. It is the *jīva*. Finally there will be *jīvabrahmaikya* (union of the two).
>
> *But why all this? Can the world exist apart from the Self?* The "I" is always *Brahman*. Its identity need not be established by logic and practice. It is enough that one realise the Self. It is always the *Brahman*.[21]

M. Hiriyanna, however, offers a slightly different interpretation of the *mahāvākya*. He writes:

> Just as the whole universe is the effect of *māyā*, the portions of the universe which constitute the accompaniments of an individual self, like the physical body and the internal organ, are regarded as derived from the *avidyā* of that particular self. Whatever distinction there appears to be between the ego and the qualified Brahman or between one ego and another, is entirely due to these differing adjuncts. In themselves, the egos are not distinct from one another or from the qualified *Brahman*. This identity of denotation of the two terms, *jīva* and the qualified *Brahman*, while their connotations are different, is the advaitic interpretation of "That thou art" (*Tat tvam asi*). It does not mean, as it is so often represented to do, that man and the qualified *Brahman* or God (to use a term which we shall soon explain) are *as such* one. Such an attitude is as blasphemous, according to Advaita, as it is according to any religion or purely theistic doctrine.[22]

---

20. *Ibid.*, p. 597
21. *Ibid.*, emphasis added.
22. M. Hiriyanna, *The Essentials of Indian Philosophy*, London: George Allen & Unwin, 1949, pp. 163-164.

Even elsewhere, when he comments on both the *mahāvākyas* — *tat tvam asi* and *ahaṁ brahmasmi* together, there is an implicit difference in the way they are understood. He writes:

> The Upaniṣads prefer to direct our attention to it through terms like *tvam* or *ahaṁ* denoting the subject, for unlike other terms they, besides dispelling all doubt about its being, afford a better clue to its nature. When such terms are combined with another like *tat* or *Brahman* in an assertive proposition like *tat tvam asi* or *ahaṁ brahma asmi*, the reference to Reality becomes ensured. For the attributes which they respectively connote of the individual and of the cosmic subject — such as the bondage of the one and the freedom of the other — being mutually incompatible, our mind abandons the explicit sense of the terms, and travels beyond those attributes to that in which they are grounded (*nirviśeṣa-vastu*) as constituting the true import of the proposition. The dropping of these attributes, we should add, signifies little because they are but illusive barriers erected by *māya* between the *jīva* and Īśvara. It should also be pointed out that we do not here identify the ground of one set of attributes with that of the other, for such identification would be meaningless without some difference equally real between them. To avoid this implication we merely deny the distinction between the two, so that what the proposition in strictness means is that the *jīva* is *not other* than *Brahman*.[23]

Another position is more literal, and, as routed through Ramaṇa, amounts to this that "*tat tvam asi* also appears as *ahaṁ brahmasmi* (I am *Brahman*)."[24]

---

23. M. Hiriyanna, *The Outlines of Indian Philosophy*, London: George Allen & Unwin, 1932, p. 374. Also see Anantanand Rambachan, *Accomplishing the Accomplished: The Vedas as a Source of Valid Knowledge in Śaṅkara*, Honolulu: University of Hawai Press, 1991, pp. 76-77.

24. Troy Wilson Organ, *op. cit.*, p. 114.

The results of the metaphorical exploration of the reflection and delimitation theories may now be considered. First, on the face of it, the delimitation approach would yield a more direct meaning of the saying *tat tvam asi* than the reflection theory. The situation becomes more complex once the point is made. The Bhāmatī school of Vācaspati Miśra both (1) accepts the delimitation theory but (2) also locates *avidyā* in the *jīvas*.[25] Although the first point suggests a more direct interpretation of *tat tvam asi* the second does not! Hiriyanna relied on this second point to establish the identity of *jīva* and Īśvara rather than *jīva* and Brahman. Third, the Vivaraṇa school of Padmapāda both (1) accepts the reflection theory and (2) locates nescience in *Brahman*.[26] It therefore consistently supports a less direct interpretation of *tat tvam asi*. Fourth, it is ironical that the Vivaraṇa school holds "that an encounter with any of the "great sayings" (*mahāvākyas*) of Advaita such as *tat tvam asi* ("thou art that") is sufficient for the attainment of enlightenment"[27] and yet seems to favour an *indirect* interpretation.[28] Finally, to complicate the situation further,

---

25. Eliot Deutsch and J.A.B. van Buitenen, *op. cit.*, p. 252.
26. *Ibid.*, p. 242.
27. *Ibid.*
28. The following classification of *mahāvākyas* is not without interest here. "Another classification of the Mahāvākyas is possible: The sentence "Knowledge is Brahman" (*prajñānam Brahma*) is a definition (*lakṣaṇa vākya*); "That Thou art" (*tat tvam asi*) is the sentence which teaches (*upadeśa vākya*); "I am Brahman" (*ahaṁ brahmāsmi*) is the sentence of practice (*anusandhāna vākya*), i.e. one should constantly try to realise the Supreme Truth by repeating this sentence over and over again so that the truth of it sinks in; "this Self is Brahman" (*ayam ātmā brahma*) is the sentence which embodies the acme of experience (*anubhava vākya*)." (K. Satchidananda Murty, *Revelation and Reason in Advaita Vedānta*, Delhi: Motilal Banarsidass, 1974, p. 75).

Śaṅkara himself uses the delimitation theory, in the context of *jīva* and Īśvara, which confirms Mahadevan's view that the metaphors had not yet become theories.[29] But it is clear that the metaphor of reflection came to favour the *jīva* = Īśvara rather than *ātman* = *Brahman* interpretation of *tat tvam asi*. Such a claim may be made on the basis of the following extract from the *Pañcapādikā* of Padmapāda, at least in terms of the doctrine of *pratibimbavāda* which will be explained in due course. Suffice it to say here that, according to this view, the *jīva* is a reflection of the divine prototype and the reflection is held to be real in its aspect of identity with the original, though not real in the form of reflection.

> XXIX, 107. Here (the opponent of the doctrine that the object and the image are identical) says — let it be conceded that there is no distinct object, but the assertion, "that alone is that" (i.e., that *pratibimba* is nothing but *bimba*) cannot be tolerated, for it is perceived that the silver (appearing) in the nacre though unreal, manifests itself as identical in nature with the real silver.
>
> It is not so. There (in the shell-silver cognition) because of the sublation it is regarded as illusory. Here no sublation of the image as such is in evidence. The disappearance of that (i.e., the image on the removal of the mirror) is not a case of sublation; for then it (sublation) would overtake the mirror also.
>
> XXIX, 108. *Pūrvapakṣin*. — Well, is not sublation evident from the sentence "That thou art?"
>
> *Siddhāntin. - Not so; there (in the sentence) "that thou (art)" what is intimated is that the individual soul (jīva) which is in the position of the image (pratibimba) is of the nature of Brahman occupying the position of the object (bimba).* Otherwise the

29. Karl H. Potter, ed., *op. cit.*, pp. 129-30, 148-49.

sentence would not be (of the form) — "that thou art" but would be "thou art not" like "silver is not. . ."

XXIX, 110. He who thinks that it is not the original (*bimba*) alone, that as existing outside itself is revealed by the visual rays which have turned back from the reflector but that the original remaining in its own place (viz. the nacre) is revealed by the rays which having impinged upon the mirror turn back and proceed in the opposite direction — him, experience itself condemns; as such his view is not controverted.[30]

---

30. Eliot Deutsch and J.A.B. Buitenen, *op. cit.*, p. 247, emphasis added.

3

The Role of Avidyā

THE central issue which gave rise to these intricacies should not be forgotten in the discussion of these intricacies — the need to explain the plurality of *jīvas* consistently with the unitary nature of the ultimate reality as pure consciousness.

The general principle in terms of which this apparent plurality was explained was that of *avidyā*, or nescience. Then the question arises: what is the locus of *avidyā*? Is *Brahman* the locus of *avidyā*, or is the *jīva* its locus, or is some intermediate entity its locus?

Four scholars have used the metaphor of reflection in a major way to explain the plurality of *jīvas* through *avidyā*. All of them regard *Brahman* as the locus of *avidyā* and working with this shared assumption work out the details in terms of the metaphor of reflection. All of them belong, in their ideological orientation on this point, to the Vivaraṇa school. These Advaitins are Sureśvara (ninth century), Sarvajñātman (tenth century), Padmapāda (ninth century) and Prakāśātman (thirteenth century).[1]

Sureśvara provides detailed arguments for why *avidyā* should be located in the Self,[2] but here we are more

---

1. • Eliot Deutsch and J.A.B. Buitenen, *op. cit.*, emphasis added, p. 313.

2. *Ibid.*, pp. 227-28.

concerned with his use of the metaphor of reflection. "The *Jīvas*, according to Sureśvara, are but reflections of *Brahman* (*cidābhāsa*) on individual *antaḥkaraṇa* (*avidyā* as mind with its *saṁskāras*). Reflection on the product of *avidyā*, (i.e. mind) is *Jīva*, and the reflection on the causal *avidyā* is Īśvara."[3] The last line should not generate the impression that according to him "*avidyā* is of two kinds"[4] or that *māyā* and *avidyā* are not identical for him. "This reflection (*pratibimba*), according to Sureśvara, being different from the original (*bimba*), is a false phenomenon (*ābhāsa*); and this has earned for the theory a new name, viz. the *ābhāsavāda*. . . So, it is the pure *cit* that runs into bondage through the *ābhāsa* (reflection) and is liberated with the destruction of the *ābhāsa*."[5]

Sureśvara's dependence on the metaphor of reflection can be seen clearly in the following verses of his *Naiśkarmyasiddhi*:

> The one seer (Self) in all being, shines as if different because of the objects, even as the sun with his wealth of rays shines as many (as reflected on account of the different water-containers.) (ii. 47)

> Just as for one and the same person the state of being friend, neutral, or foe is imagined by other people, so also, of the pure consciousness which is non-different, difference is dependent on the internal organ. (ii. 48)

---

3. Dinesh Chandra Bhattacharya, "Post-Śaṅkara Advaita," in Haridas Bhattacharyya, ed., *The Cultural Heritage of India*, Calcutta: The Ramakrishna Mission Institute of Culture, 1953, Vol. III, p. 261.
4. *Ibid.*, 259.
5. *Ibid.*, 260.

> Just as for the sun there is complete appropriation by the water-vessels, for the Self, because of the intellects, there is attainment of their activity, shape and space. (ii. 49)[6]

Sarvajñātman, a follower of Sureśvara, goes further. Like Sureśvara, he also subscribes to the reflection-theory, otherwise known as *ābhāsavāda*. *Māyā* (nescience), according to Sarvajñātman,

> is one and not many. It pervades all the individuals (*jīva*s) and it continues to exist even after a single individual's ignorance is destroyed through realization, just as a universal (*jāti*, e.g. cowhood) pervades all the existent individuals and is not affected by any change in their number. The *jīva*s are reflections of *Brahman* on *antaḥkaraṇa*s (minds) while the reflection of *Brahman* on *māyā* (*avidyā*) is Īśvara. *Māyā*, through its *āvaraṇa Śakti* (concealing power) and *vikṣepa Śakti* (transforming power), makes it possible for *Brahman*, its only object and support, to appear as the *Jīva*, Īśvara, and the world.[7]

Sarvajñātman also raises another issue and attempts to answer it.

> It may be asked how *avidyā* can superimpose itself and its products on the Self. Should there not be another *avidyā* to connect the previous one to the Self? We reply: just as in some philosophical schools difference is stated to differentiate the relate as well as itself from them, for superimposing

---

6. Quoted in T.M.P. Mahadevan, *Superimposition in Advaita Vedānta*, New Delhi: Sterling Publishers Private Ltd., 1985, p. 25. The following verse may also be of interest: "Just as the movement of clouds is superimposed on the moon on account of delusion, even so, being happy, etc. which are the attributes of the intellect are thought to be in the Self." (ii.101)

7. Dinesh Chandra Bhattacharya, *op. cit.*, vol. III, p. 261.

> *avidyā* on the Self there is no need for another *avidyā*. The objects superimposed by *avidyā* on the Self are removed when *avidyā* itself is destroyed through knowledge of the Self.[8]

The other model based on the metaphor of reflection was developed by Padmapāda. Padmapāda utilizes two metaphors of reflection — of the red crystal and the mirror, and then establishes the greater appropriateness of one over the other in detailing his cosmic cartography. Karl H. Potter explains:

> Padmapāda is the first of our authors to work out in detail a "map" of the process of creation. In a remarkable passage he presents it quite explicitly for us. *Avidyā* (the list of synonyms is informative) veils the natural awareness of *Brahman*, and the result is a transformation (*pariṇāma*) of that *avidyā* which has God as its locus and which is termed *ahaṁkāra*, the sense of ego, of awareness, agency, and enjoyership. This *ahaṁkāra* is not, however, an evolute of *prakṛti* or *avidyā*, since this would make it completely different from the Self; rather, it is falsely attributed to the Self as a crystal is falsely held to possess red colour because it is near the flower. The analogue of the flower, according to Padmapāda, is the internal organ (*antaḥkaraṇa*), that is, the *buddhi*.
>
> Padmapāda proceeds to contrast the analogy of the red crystal with that part of the process which is like reflection in a mirror. The difference is that in the case of the red crystal the crystal's nature (its color) is different from that of the flower, so that our error comes in identifying them, but in the case of the face in the mirror the prototype is identical with its reflection, the reflected face is not different from the face. And the mirror reflection model is ultimately the right

8. T.M.P. Mahadevan, *Superimposition in Advaita Vedānta.*

> one, Padmapāda concludes. The ego is identical with *Brahman*, not just similar to it. There is a lengthy dialogue to prove this important point of identity, to show that the *jīva* has the same nature as *Brahman*, even though, like the face and its reflection, they appear in different places.[9]

If by substituting the mirror-image something is gained, then by eliminating the crystal-image something is lost. The metaphorical gains and losses involved in this substitution may be weighed as follows:

> An implication of Padmapāda's analysis is that when one appreciates the identity of *jīva* and *Brahman* it does not follow that the medium — the internal organ — is destroyed, any more than it is the case that when one realizes that one's face is identical with its reflection in the mirror the mirror is thereby destroyed. This is handy, for it explains why upon liberation the *jīva* does not immediately disappear. When pressed about this with the objection that his model required a distinct, separate medium, Padmapāda immediately has recourse to the rope-snake analogy, or alternatively, the pot-space analogy. In both the latter cases, the prototype (analogous to *Brahman*) is not related to the rest of the items in the model (analogous to the adjuncts, including the medium).
>
> Padmapāda, however, is constrained to confess that after all none of the models is quite sufficient to completely explain the mystery of creation. Later Advaitins continue to explore these models with the hope that they can ultimately be shown to resolve the mystery.[10]

Prakāśātman is a later day follower of Padmapāda. According to him:

---

9. Karl H. Potter, ed., *op. cit.*, p. 261.
10. *Ibid.*, p. 87.

> The *jīvas* . . . are but images of *Brahman* reflected on *avidyā* as *antaḥkaraṇa* (mind) and *saṁskāra* (mind in a causal condition). The reflected images, according to Padmapāda and Prakāśātman, are not different from the original (*bimba*) *Brahman* and are therefore real as *Brahman*, though not real in the form of reflected images. This theory of reflection is called the *Pratibimbavāda* as contrasted with the *Ābhāsavāda* of Sureśvara. But Īśvara is not a reflection, as Sureśvara holds, but *Brahman* in the aspect of being the original (*bimba-caitanya*) of reflections which constitute the *jīvas*.[11]

The last sentence reinforces the point already made, that the *bimba-pratibimba* variety of the reflection metaphor modifies the interpretation of the *mahāvākya* : *tat tvam asi*. In any case:

> Another important point is that there is no antagonism between avidyā and self-shining *Brahman*, which is the locus and the revealer of *avidyā* (*ajñānāvabhāsaka*). It is the knowledge of Brahman (*Brahmajñāna*) which is antagonistic to and destructive of *avidyā*. Though *avidyā* is one, the *jīvas* are many owing to the plurality of *antaḥkaraṇas* which are the adjuncts of the *jīvas*. Prakāśātman holds a long discussion on the theory of reflection (*pratibimbavāda*) which he supports in preference to the *avacchedavāda* (the theory of limitation) which he refutes with sound arguments that have been accepted by most of the later Advaitins.[12]

Vācaspati Misra is normally taken as the representative of the other school opposed to the reflection-theory, namely, the delimitation-theory. It may be worth remarking, however, that although Vācaspati is more inclined to the theory of limitation (*avacchedavāda*) with regard to the appearance of

---

11. Dinesh Chandra Bhattacharya, *op. cit.*, p. 264.
12. *Ibid.*, p. 265..

the *Jīvas*, in Bhāmatī, "Vācaspati has described the *jīvas* as reflections also. On this point his view may be regarded as syncretic as in the case of Śaṅkara. But Appaya Dīkṣitar, in his *Parimala*, holds that Vācaspati is in favour of the theory of reflection, which, according to him, is the final import of the *Brahma-Sūtra*."[13] As we are concerned only with the metaphor of reflection here we will not pursue the rival theory beyond making three points. We shall begin by stating with maximum plausibility the case for the *pratibimba* view, then notice its main criticism by its opponents and finally close with a comment on the *ābhāsavāda* version of the reflection metaphor.

What is broadly labelled the *vivaraṇa* view of the matter may be stated as follows:

> Thus, followers of the Vivaraṇa school claimed that the reflection of a prototype in a mirror most accurately represents the nature of the association of absolute consciousness with ignorance because this metaphor emphasizes the non-difference of the reflected image, or modified consciousness, from the prototype, or *ātman*. These *pratibimbavādins* argued that the reflection of an image in a mirror requires neither an impression on, nor a transformation of, the mirror itself. Rather, the true location of the reflection is the prototype, just as the locus of the illusory self is absolute consciousness. Further, these thinkers maintained that this metaphor allowed them to attribute individual differences in the potential for intellectual discrimination and spiritual sensitivity to the degree of ignorance into which the absolute is reflected, just as the reflection of an object in water varies according to the clarity and calmness of the water.[14]

---

13. *Ibid*. p. 267.

14. William M. Indich, *Consciousness in Advaita Vedānta*, Delhi: Motilal Banarsidass, 1980, p. 52.

The basic criticism the metaphor attracted was that "the metaphor of reflection failed to explain how absolute consciousness, which has no sensible qualities, can be reflected."[15]

There seems to be a slight tendency to neglect the *ābhāsavāda* version of the metaphor of reflection in some circles. Thus Indich tucks it away with the remark that a "third position, Sureśvara's *ābhāsavāda*, was also suggested in this context, but as it is actually a subtle variation of the *pratibimbavāda* position it need not concern us here."[16] Modern Advaitins, both scholars and practitioners, attach more importance to Sureśvara's views. T.M.P. Mahadevan discusses his view in considerable detail[17] while Ramana's descriptions are often suggestive of it:

> The waking, dream and sleep states have their origin in the Original Darkness (*mūlā avidyā*). With the mind outgoing and deriving experiences from its modes in the waking and dream states, and indrawn in sleep, experiencing with modes of *māyā*, a unique power regulates all activities of the individuals and of the universe. All these are only phenomena passing through the Reflected Light, on the substratum of the Self-radiant Being.

> Just as a rope-snake cannot be seen in broad daylight, nor rope itself in thick darkness, so also the world appears neither in the *samādhi* state of Self-shining pure Being or in deep sleep, swoon, etc. Only in Reflected Light (Light mixed with Darkness or knowledge soiled by Ignorance) can the world, *not independent of its Source*, seem to rise up, flourish and be resolved. Its diversity too cannot be exclusive of the Reality,

---

15. *Ibid.*
16. *Ibid.*, p. 52 note 1.
17. T.M.P. Mahadevan, *Superimposition in Advaita Vedānta*, p. 26 ff.

> the original Source. Here a play is going on in which the One Single Being becomes manifold, is objectified and then withdrawn. There must be Śakti (power) to do it, and wonderful too! She cannot also be independent of Her origin. In the Self-shining Pure Being this Śakti cannot be seen. Nevertheless, Her actions are only too well-known. How sublime![18]

The reflected light of consciousness referred to in the passage is none other than *ābhāsa*.[19]

One point in the application of the metaphor of reflection in relation to the appearance of the *jīva*s awaits clarification. The confusion on this point can be identified in the following two back-to-back accounts of the emergence of the *jīva*s in the *Advaita-Bodha-Dīpikā*:

> 77. D.: If the Supreme Self had by joining the I-mode of the mind become the illusory *jīva* he should appear as a single *jīva*. But there are many *jīva*s. How can the single Reality manifest as innumerable *jīva*s?
>
> 78-80. M.: As soon as the illusion of a single *jīva* becomes operative in the Pure Supreme Self, it naturally begets other illusory *jīva*s in the Pure Ether of Knowledge. If a dog enters a room walled by mirrors, it first gives rise to one reflection in one mirror which by a series of reflections becomes innumerable and the dog finding itself surrounded by so many other dogs growls and shows fright. So it is with the Self of pure, non-dual Ether of Consciousness, the illusion of one *jīva* is perforce associated with illusion of several *jīva*s.

---

18. *Talks with Śrī Ramaṇa Maharṣi*, pp. 287-88, diacritics supplied.
19. *Ibid.*, p. 75. The discussions on these issues after a point get unbearably complex. P.T. Raju combines concise survey with judicious assessment in his treatment of the subject (*op. cit.*, pp. 117-20).

> 81-83. Again, the habit of seeing the world as you-I, he etc. forces the dreamer to see similar illusory entities in dreams also. Similarly the accumulated habits of past births make the Self which is only pure Knowledge-Ether see numberless illusory *jivas* even now. What can be beyond the scope of *māyā* which is itself inscrutable?[20]

In traditional Advaitin jargon: according to verses 78-80 it is Īśvara who is reflected in the various *jīvas* and according to verses 81-83 it is *Brahman*. The position implicit in verses 78-80 may be elaborated either by claiming "that there is only one chief *jīva* called *hiraṇyagarbha*, and that the many are his reflections"[21] or by claiming, if the first *jīva* is identified with Īśvara that both Īśvara and *jīva* are reflections and Īśvara is a prototype of the reflection — a theoretical possibility not mentioned in the general literature on the subject.[22]

The position adopted in verses 81-83 reflects the adoption of what P.T. Raju calls the "finally true view" in the welter of the various theories, namely, that "the *Brahman* and the *jīva* are the same. Only, the former forgets its true nature and so regards itself as finite; but the moment the *jīva* knows his true nature, he becomes the *Brahman*."[23] The use of the dream analogy provides the clue here in the *Advaita-Bodha-Dīpikā* as it ties into a section of verse 100:

> M.: All this universe is the dream-product of the non-dual, untainted, Knowledge-Bliss only.
>
> D.: But a dream can happen only in sleep. Has the Supreme Self gone to sleep in order to see this dream?

---

20. Sri Ramanananda Saraswathi, tr., *op. cit.*, p. 14.
21. P.T. Raju, *op. cit.*, p. 119.
22. *Ibid.*, p. 118.
23. *Ibid.*

M.: Our sleep corresponds to Its Ignorance which hides Its real nature from time immemorial. So It dreams the dream of this universe. Just as the dreamer is deluded into thinking himself the experiencer of his dreams, so also the unchanging Self is by illusion presented as a *jīva* experiencing this *saṁsāra*.

101. On seeing the dreamlike body, senses, etc., the *jīva* is deluded into the belief that he is the body, senses, etc., with them he turns round and round through the waking, dream and deep sleep states. This forms his *saṁsāra*.[24]

---

24. Sri Ramananda Sarasvathi, tr., *op. cit.*, p. 17.

4

Some Conclusions Based on Traditional Views

Some broad conclusions can now be suggested on the basis of the historical survey of the previous sections. One of them is the obvious point that the metaphor of reflection is virtually universal in its usage — in any case it is well-represented in the religious and cultural traditions of Asia. This is so on account of its versatility. It can illustrate the properties of the mind, the spirit or even pure consciousness.

The metaphor has been especially significant within the bounds of Advaita Vedānta in establishing the relationship between *Brahman-Ātman* and *Jīva* — or more simply — between Absolute and Modified Consciousness. As the discussion of theme was fairly persistent it seems possible to draw certain conclusions from it.

The first major conclusion which suggests itself is the role of the metaphors in understanding the "great sayings" or *mahāvākya*s of the Upaniṣads — more particularly the *mahāvākya*: *tat tvam asi* or that thou art.

It is possible to suggest here that the *ābhāsavāda* version of the theory[1] is perhaps as direct as the delimitation theory and certainly more direct than the *bimba-pratibimbavāda* version in relating the *jīva* with *Brahman*. This is one of the more

1. Sureśvara's discussion of the *mahāvākya*.

interesting points to emerge from the discussion, as although on the face of it the delimitation theory should apparently produce the most direct result, the advocacy of the plurality of nescience, and not just the *jīva*s, seems to complicate the situation. Thus the metaphor of reflection itself becomes a matter for some reflection, especially as to how the original prototype arises in the case of *bimba-pratibimbavāda* and how it is to be understood in the case of *avacchedavāda*.[2]

The second major conclusion pertains to the psychological predispositions the metaphorical orientations create in terms of the form of idealism to which a sub-school of Advaita might be inclined to subscribe. It has been argued, for instance, that "by maintaining *Brahman* and not the *jīva*s, to be the locus of *avidyā*, Sureśvara has carefully opposed the tendency towards subjective idealism."[3] But this may have prepared the ground for the subsequent formulation of the doctrine of *ekajīvavāda* by Prakāśānanda!

> The seeming plurality of *jīva*s is due to the plurality of bodies. The one infinite Self, which is of the nature of self-luminous consciousness and bliss, has imagined itself to be a worldly *jīva* through its own ignorance. When, again, this *jīva* hankers after freedom, it resorts to the prescribed means of *śravaṇa*, etc. all imaginary as in a dream, and regains its real state of freedom by destroying its ignorance. Then, of course, no other *jīva* or the world remains. Thus, Prakāśānanda supports *ekajīvavāda* (the "soleity" or oneness of the *jīva*) as the basis of his extreme form of subjective idealism (*dṛṣṭi-sṛṣṭi-vāda*).[4]

---

2. For attempts at answers to these questions as well on the range of views involved, see P.T. Raju, *The Idealistic Thought of India*, London: George Allen & Unwin, 1953, p. 114 ff.
3. Dinesh Chandra Bhattacharya, *op. cit.*, p. 259.
4. *Ibid.*, p. 276.

However, Prakāśānanda inclined towards the Vivaraṇa school, and it seems apparent that *dṛṣṭi-sṛṣṭi-vāda* (as distinguished from the *eka-jīvavāda*) connects more naturally with the Bhāmatī school of Vacaspati. "According to some interpreters (e.g. Madhusūdana in his *Siddhānta-bindu*), Vacaspati's view is a type of subjective idealism, the *jīva*s, with *avidyā* abiding in them, being the material cause of the world, which is different for each individual."[5] Although some traditional scholars have demurred, there seems to be little doubt that:

> there are certain elements in Vacaspati's views which tend towards some sort of [subjective] idealism. His advocacy of the plurality of nescience and of the *jīva*s as the loci of nesciences leads to the plurality of the world — a different world for each *jīva*. Thus for the different *jīva*s there are different worlds, though they are similar to a great extent. It is owing to this similarity that the experiences of different individuals are similar, though the objects are different.[6]

Three important points are interacting here: (1) that both the Vivaraṇa and the Bhāmatī schools are capable of generating subjective idealism; (2) that because of their metaphorical orientation this tends to lead to *ekajīvavāda* in the context of Vivaraṇa and — if I may be permitted to coin an expression — to *pratyekajīvavāda* in the context of the Bhāmatī school and (3) that *ekajivavāda* and *dṛṣṭi-sṛṣṭi-vāda* should be clearly distinguished from one another, which does not seem to have always been the case.[7]

---

5. *Ibid.*, p. 266.
6. *Ibid.*
7. Eliot Deutsch and J.A.B. Buitenan, *op. cit.*, p. 224.

A third major conclusion which emerges is that given the non-dual *ātman* the question of the plurality of *jīva*s remains to be accounted for in a rationally satisfactory manner, if that is possible. There is a tendency among both Advaitin thinkers and sages to become heuristic at this point. T.M.P. Mahadevan writes for instance:

> The truth of Advaita is admittedly beyond the reach of speech and mind. The teacher can only point to it employing halting words and inadequate ideas. The mode and manner of his teaching will depend upon the competence of the student concerned. That is why in the exposition of Advaita we find the entire gamut of philosophical perspectives from near-realism to extreme subjectivism. In the Vivaraṇa for instance, in which the theory of a single *jīva* is explained in one place, the disciple is made to ask "Who is that single *jīva*?" and the teacher simply replies "You are that *jīva*." In the *Saṁkṣepaśārīraka* in one context the *ekajīvavāda* (the theory of one *jīva*) is adopted, while in some other places *nānā-jīva-vāda* (the theory of a plurality of *jīva*s) is maintained. The sole aim of the Advaita teachers is to lead the aspirants of different grades to the ultimate truth of the non-dual Self.[8]

And Ramaṇa Maharṣi, in an extended passage runs the gamut from *ābhāsavāda* to *pratibimbavāda* through to *ekajīvavāda* with presumably *avaccedavāda* to be read between the lines. He writes:

> Multiplicity of individuals is a moot point with most persons. A *jīva* is only the light reflected on the ego. The person identifies himself with the ego and argues that there must be more like him. He is not easily convinced of the absurdity of his position. Does a man who sees many

8. T.M.P. Mahadevan, *Superimposition in Advaita Vedānta*, pp. 50-51.

individuals in his dream persist in believing them to be real and enquire after them when he wakes up?

This argument does not convince the disputant.

Again, there is the moon. Let any one look at her from any place at any time; she is the same moon. Everyone knows it. Now suppose that there are several receptacles of water reflecting the moon herself. If one of the receptacles falls to pieces, that reflection disappears. Its disappearance does not affect the real moon or the other reflections. It is similar with an individual attaining Liberation. He alone is liberated.

The sectarian of multiplicity makes this his argument against non-duality. "If the Self is single, if one man is liberated, that means that all souls are liberated. In practice it is not so. Therefore Advaita is not correct."

The weakness in the argument is that the reflected light of the Self is mistaken for the original Light of the Self. The ego, the world and the individuals are all due to the person's *vāsanā*s. When they perish, that person's hallucinations disappear, that is to say one pitcher is broken and the relative reflection is at an end.

The fact is that the Self is never bound. There can therefore be no Release for It. All the troubles are for the ego only.

A question was asked why it was wrong to say that there is a multiplicity of *jīva*s. *Jīva*s are certainly many. For a *jīva* is only the ego and forms the reflected light of the Self. Multiplicity of selves may be wrong but not of *jīva*s.

M.: *Jīva* is called so because he sees the world. A dreamer sees many *jīva*s in a dream but all of them are not real. The dreamer alone exists and he sees all. So it is with the individual and the world. There is the creed of only one Self which is also called the creed of only one *jīva*. It says that the *jīva* is only one who sees the whole world and the *jīva*s therein.

D.: Then *jīva* means the Self here.

M.: So it is. But the Self is not a seer. But here he is said to see the world. So he is differentiated as the *jīva*.[9]

Elsewhere he also resorts to *pratbimbavāda* and *ābhāsavāda* in quick succession, without establishing the greater appropriateness of one over the other but using both not for aetiological but soteriological purposes. In the course of this exposition he does not establish the superiority of one metaphor over the other but rather, in both cases, the superiority of his own *direct* method over other indirect methods. In the following passage the *pratibimbavāda* model is utilised:

> Some Upaniṣads also speak of 101 *nāḍīs* which spread from the heart, one of them being the vital *nāḍī*. If the *jīva* comes down from above and gets reflected in the brain, as the yogis say, there must be a reflecting surface in action. That must also be capable of limiting the Infinite Consciousness to the limits of the body. In short the Universal Being becomes limited as a *jīva*. Such reflecting medium is furnished by the aggregate of the *vāsanā*s of the individual. It acts like the water in a pot which reflects the image of an object. If the pot be drained of its water there will be no reflection. The object will remain without being reflected. The object here is the Universal Being-Consciousness which is all-pervading and therefore immanent in all. It need not be cognised by reflection alone; it is self-resplendent. Therefore the seeker's aim must be to drain away the *vāsanā*s from the heart and let not reflecting medium obstruct the Light of Eternal Consciousness. This is achieved by the search for the origin of the ego and by diving into the heart. This is the direct method for Self-Realisation. One who

9. *Talks with Śrī Ramaṇa Maharṣi*, p. 530.

> adopts it need not worry about *nāḍīs*, the brain, the *suṣumnā*, the *paranāḍī*, the *kuṇḍalini*, *prāṇāyāma* or the six centres.[10]

This is immediately followed by a passage which utilizes the *ābhāsavāda* model:

> The self does not come from anywhere else and enter the body through the crown of the head. It is as it is, ever sparkling, ever steady, unmoving and unchanging. The changes which are noticed are not inherent in the Self which abides in the Heart and is self-luminous like the Sun. The changes are seen in Its Light. The relation between the Self and the body or the mind may be compared to that of a clear crystal and its background. If the crystal is placed against a red flower, it shines red; if placed against a green leaf it shines green, and so on. The individual confines himself to the limits of the changeful body or of the mind which derives its existence from the unchanging Self. All that is necessary is to give up this mistaken identity, and that done, the ever-shining Self will be seen to be the single non-dual Reality.[11]

All this is, of course, in keeping with the standard view within Advaita that such metaphors of doctrines possess only instrumental and not intrinsic values. For instance:

> Madhusūdana supports many of the conflicting theories separately and independently, implying thereby that any of the theories may be resorted to in explaining the indeterminable false world, the main interest of the Advaitins being in the one absolute *Brahman*. Thus he analyses and accepts the unity as well as the plurality of the *jīvas*, the unity as well as the plurality of nesciences, *Brahman* as well as the *jīva* as the locus of nescience, the objectivity of the world as well as the Vedāntic solipsism (*dṛṣṭi-sṛṣṭi-vāda*), and so on. He

---

10. *Ibid.*, p. 576.
11. *Ibid.*, p. 576.

prescribes the different theories for different Vedānta students according to their fitness (*adhikāra*).[12]

All this is no doubt admirable in its own way but it does render the task of the metaphorical mapping much more difficult than it might be otherwise.

12. Dinesh Chandra Bhattacharya, *op. cit.*, p. 27.

5

The Metaphor of Reflection in a Modern Setting

THERE is a tendency among some modern Advaitins to employ astronomical metaphors to explain certain Advaitic doctrines, which might otherwise remain more obscure or opaque. Some of the illustrations used by M. Hiriyanna are of this kind, and are worth examining. They set the scene for the use of the metaphor of reflection in a very different context. M. Hiriyanna writes, while presenting Śaṅkara's critique of the *bhedābheda* of Bhartṛprapañca, that according to Śaṅkara:

> the doctrine merely restates in a new form the problem to be solved. It holds that creation means only the potential becoming the actual; but this distinction between the potential and the actual is purely verbal, and does not really solve the problem of causation. The view of this school is that sameness (*abheda*) and difference (*bheda*), so far from being incompatible, are intelligible only if taken together, while Śaṅkara maintains that, being mutually contradictory, they cannot be predicted as one and the same thing. It makes the nature of the thing self-contradictory; and self-contradiction, according to him, points to falsity. In other words, if unity and diversity be each an abstraction taken separately according to the one school, their combination *also* is so according to the other. Reality is what transcends

> both and, at the same time, explains them. To cite an illustration which is as old as the Upaniṣads: *It is like the sun which explains the phenomena of day and night, but at the same time transcends them in that it knows no night, nor even day in our sense of the term.*[1]

In fact the illustration can be used to explain much more. *Brahman* is said to be beyond good and evil just as the sun is beyond day and night. But if we had to refer to the sun in terms of its similarity to day and night, which of the two would we choose? Obviously day. This helps explain how Advaita can in the same breath ontologically claim that *Brahman* is beyond good and evil and morally recommend good over evil.

M. Hiriyanna resorts to an astronomical illustration in another context. The context is provided by Śaṅkara's claim that liberation "is not a state to be newly gained, but is the very nature of the self." Hence "we can hardly speak of a means in its ordinary sense for achieving it." He goes on to say:

> We might illustrate the point equally well by referring to the distinction between a solar and a lunar eclipse. In the latter, the light of the sun is actually cut off from the moon by the earth coming between it and the sun, so that the passing off of the eclipse signifies a real change in the condition of the moon, viz. the part that was enveloped in darkness becoming lit. In a solar eclipse, on the other hand, the luminary continues to be during the eclipse exactly as it was before or will be afterwards. It only appears to be eclipsed because the intervening moon prevents it from being seen as it really is. The re-emergence of the bright sun accordingly means

---

1. M. Hiriyanna, *The Essentials of Indian Philosophy*, p. 154, emphasis added.

> no change whatsoever in it, but only a moving farther away of the moon or the removal of the obstacle preventing the sun from showing itself as it is. Similarly in the case of advaitic *mokṣa*, all that is needed is a removal of the obstacle that keeps the truth concealed from us and the discipline that is prescribed is solely with a view to bring about this result. It is therefore only in a negative or indirect sense that we can talk of attaining *mokṣa* here.[2]

The point is well taken. It is, therefore, not without interest that Ramaṇa also employs the metaphor of reflection in an astronomical context. Ramaṇa often compares the mind to the moon. The following passage explains the metaphor in some detail:

> Bhagavan further explained: The Self is the Heart. The Heart is self-luminous. Light arises from the Heart and reaches the brain which is the seat of the mind. The world is seen with the mind, that is, by the reflected light of the Self. It is perceived with the aid of the mind. When the mind is illumined, it is not aware of the world. If the mind is turned in towards the source of light, objective knowledge ceases. The Self alone shines forth as the Heart.
>
> The moon shines by the reflected light of the sun. When the sun has set, the moon is useful for revealing objects. When the sun has risen, no one needs the moon, although the pale disc of the moon is visible in the sky.
>
> So it is with the mind and the Heart. The mind is useful because of its reflected light. It is used for seeing objects. When it is turned inwards, the source of illumination shines forth by itself, and the mind remains dim and useless like the moon in day-time.[3]

---

2. M. Hiriyanna, *The Outlines of Indian Philosophy*, p. 378. Also see *The Essentials of Indian Philosophy*, pp. 169-70.
3. *Talks with Śrī Ramaṇa Maharṣi*, p. 94.

In terms of this metaphor the state of the mind of the Realized one is described by Ramaṇa as follows:

> See the moon and also the cloud in the sky. There is no difference in their brilliance. The moon looks only like a speck of cloud. *The jñānī's mind is like this moon before sunlight. It is there but not shining of itself.*[4]

It is said to be "before sunlight" because it "has been turned towards the source of light."

The inclusion of the next passage requires some explanation. It explains how one can speak of experiencing happiness in deep sleep. This happiness cannot be the result of *karma* according to Advaita: "pleasure produced by meritorious acts from past lives . . . that is absent in deep sleep. The passage does not deny that bliss is present, for bliss is the very nature of things, as the Upaniṣad asserts that abundance, that is, Brahman, is bliss."[5]

How then is the bliss of *ātman* experienced in pure sleep? If the analogy of the mind with the moon is kept in view, then the explanation at the end of the passage becomes suggestive:

> If pure, how is He to be experienced by means of the impure "I"? A man says "I slept happily." Happiness was his experience. If not, how could he speak of what he had not experienced? How did he experience happiness in sleep, if the Self was pure? Who is it that speaks of that experience now? *The speaker is the vijñānātmā (ignorant self) and he speaks of prajñānātmā (pure self). How can that hold?* Was this *vijñānātmā* present in sleep? His present statement of the experience of happiness in

---

4. *Ibid.*, p. 435, emphasis added.
5. Karl H. Potter, ed., *op. cit.*, p. 269.

> sleep makes one infer his existence in sleep. How then did he remain? Surely not as in the waking state. He was there very subtly. *Exceedingly subtle vijñānātmā experiences the happy prajñānātmā by means of māyā mode. It is like the rays of the moon seen below the branches, twigs and leaves of a tree.*[6]

"The point to note here is that the *ātman* is *sat*, *cit* and *ānanda*. During sleep when it is shrouded in *māyā*, its cit aspect suffers an eclipse"[7] but not its *sat* and *ānanda* aspects. The existence of the *ānanda* aspect was evoked metaphorically above by Ramaṇa. The existence of the *sat* aspect in the state of deep sleep is celebrated in the seventh verse of the Śrī *Dakṣiṇāmūrtistotra* with the help of an astronomical metaphor involving the image of an eclipsing shadow. The verse is paraphrased below:

> There is distinct cognition of gross and subtle objects respectively in *jāgrat* and in *svapna*. But during sleep, when the dream is over, there is no sense-organ activity, and there is a stillness of the mind, *manolaya*. So there is no discriminative awareness of objects. There is no *viśeṣajñāna* because the sense-organs have subsided into their activating causes. Is the *cit* which is the *ātman* present then? Does it shine? Yes; says the *śloka*. It does in the same way as the sun and moon do during an eclipse, not brightly however, but hidden by the eclipsing agent. Though the sun and moon are invisible during the eclipse, we infer their continued existence abiding before, during and after the eclipse. We say that during the eclipse the sun was the same that it was before and that it shines after it is over. Even so, in the case of the man who sleeps, his *cit* is shrouded by *māyā*. When he wakes up from his sleep, he

---

6. *Talks with Śrī Ramaṇa Maharṣi*, p. 275, emphasis added.
7. P. Sankaranarayanan, *What is Advaita*?, Bombay (Mumbai): Bharatiya Vidya Bhavan, 1970, pp. 231-32.

> establishes in his consciousness a continuity of his personal identity before, during and after sleep. This he gives expression to when, on waking from his sleep, he says: I slept happily; I did not know anything. The awareness of self-identity is called *pratyabhijñā*. To Śrī Dakṣiṇāmūrti who is the Supreme Self with whom this *pratyabhijñā* is associated, I make this salutation.[8]

What is the exact nature of sleep? And how is it different from *samādhi*? These issues of Advaitin psychology and soteriology will be pursued in the chapters that follow.

8. *Ibid.*, pp. 229-30.

6

Sleep, Samādhi and the Metaphor of the Image

Soteriological Issues

THE metaphor of image is helpful pedagogically in explaining certain ideas and concepts connected with Advaita Vedānta, which are associated with each other and are yet distinct. Consider, for instance, the phenomena of deep sleep and *samādhi*. In both these states it is claimed that the distinction between the subject and the object is overcome — then what is the difference between the two? Moreover, identity also persists through deep sleep and *samādhi*. "There is the continuity of "I" in deep slumber and in *samādhi*. Otherwise after sleep a man would get up as somebody else."[1] Several approaches have been adopted in Advaita towards answering this vital question. (1) One approach has been to represent the situation from the point of view of the *antaḥkaraṇa* or the internal organ. Various aspects of the *antaḥkaraṇa* have been referred to as *manas* (sense-mind), *buddhi* (discrimination), *ahaṁkāra* (egoism), *citta* (memory), etc.[2] In deep sleep all these aspects of the internal organ cease to function, including the

---

1. Swami Sri Ramanananda Saraswathi, tr., *op. cit.*, p. 121.
2. William M. Indich, *op. cit.*, p. 86, etc. Karl H. Potter, ed., *op. cit.*, p. 330.

ego[3] *except citta* or memory. Upon waking the re-emergent ego unites with this memory aspect and is able to claim "I slept." (2) Another approach examines the question from the point of view of *avidyā*. According to the standard Vedāntic point of view, the *jīva consists of three bodies — the physical body* (*sthūla śarīra*), the subtle body (*sūkṣma śarīra* or *liṅga śarīra*) and the causal body (*kāraṇa śarīra*). The waking state is characterised by the presence of the *sthūla śarīra*, the dreaming state by the presence of the *sūkṣma śarīra* and the deep sleep state by the presence of the *kāraṇa śarīra* or the causal body. As M. Hiriyanna explains:

> If the internal organ functions by itself in dreams unaided by the senses, that also becomes latent in sleep. Of the two elements that make up the *jīva*, one, viz. the *antaḥkaraṇa*, is lost in its cause *māyā* or, to state it more definitely, in that part or aspect of it called *avidyā* which constitutes the adjunct of individual *jīvas*. What endures then is the *sākṣin* plus *avidyā* which is known as the *kāraṇa-śarīra* or the "radical adjunct" of the self as distinguished from its subtle body (*liṅga śarīra*). Consequently there is in sleep no subject at all as such and no states of consciousness as in dreams or waking. This makes the "experience" of dreamless sleep quite unique, though occurring normally and almost universally. What we have in that condition is the *sākṣin* — not the *jīva* — associated with its own *avidyā*, in which the internal organ has provisionally merged. In this state also, we must remember, individuality persists; but the individuality then is due to the union of the *sākṣin* with *avidyā* and not with the internal organ.[4]

(3) Another approach is to describe the state from the point of view of the *ātman*. From this point of view four key points

---

3. Karl H. Potter, ed., *op. cit.*, p. 326.
4. M. Hiriyanna, *The Outlines of Indian Philosophy*, p. 348.

need to be considered: (i) that the experience of sleep is blissful; (ii) that during the experience of sleep there is no awareness of the experience; (iii) that despite lack of such awareness, the sense of identity with the pre-sleep person is not lost but that; (iv) apparently in sleep one is empirically unconscious.

The fourth point may be answered first, namely, that sleep seems to be an unconscious state. Śaṅkara counters this objection by claiming that "the absence of knowledge in deep sleep is the consequence of the absence of anything experienced separate from consciousness, rather than the absence of consciousness itself."[5] Once deep sleep has in some sense been established as a conscious experience, the logical (as distinguished from the scriptural or phenomeno-logical) assertion of its blissful nature is based on the Advaitin's claim to have a reflective cognition or memory of blissful sleep experience upon waking. The Advaitin argues on the one hand that it would be absurd for him to try to claim that he perceives the blissful experience of sleep while it takes place, since he has already claimed that the senses and the other means of knowledge are inactive in this state. On the other hand, however, he argues that the immediate awareness of the blissful nature of sleep-experience realized when we awaken cannot derive from an inference based on contrasting our memory of having been in a state of disquieted knowledge prior to sleep with the peacefulness accompanying waking. He thus concludes that the blissful absence of suffering was actually revealed or presented in sleep, although it was not perceived as such until the knowing mind was reactivated upon waking.[6]

---

5. William Indich, *op. cit.*, p. 98.
6. *Ibid.*, p. 104.

The remaining two points have been clarified by M. Hiriyanna as follows:

> The *avidyā* operates in sleep only partially. It obscures the true character of reality, but does not split it up into a variety of "names" and "forms" as in dreams or in waking, since the discontinuous and mutually excluding *vṛttis* of the internal organ are absent there. The experience of sleep involves a reference to both these elements — continuance of personality and absence of all variety — as is shown by the latter reminiscence that one was asleep and did not know anything. Over and above these there is felt in sleep bliss which, according to a fundamental postulate of the system, is the very nature of the self and which, owing to the absence of all distractions then, becomes manifest. This unalloyed happiness survives even waking, as shown by the state of repose that continues for a while; but it disappears as man lapses back into the vortex of common life — a belief which is Wordsworthian in its character. "All beings visit that Brahma-world day after day, but not one realizes it." None of these features of sleep, it must be noted, is "known" at the time, for no knowledge, whether mediate or immediate, is possible in the absence of the internal organ. But they are nevertheless realized then as shown by the fact of their being recalled afterwards.[7]

(4) A fourth approach is a heuristic one. It is to regard deep sleep as constituting an experience not of, but analogous to, that of the *ātman*. In fact this analogy is even preferred by some to the analogy of bridal mysticism:

> Thus, when selecting an analogy for the experience of bliss, the Advaitin rejects love, which entails a struggle to overcome the separation between two beings and chooses dreamless sleep instead. The Advaitin sees three reasons for the superiority of

---

7. M. Hiriyanna, *The Outlines of Indian Philosophy*, pp. 348-49.

this choice. First, deep sleep is a natural condition which involves neither struggle nor attainment. Second, the bliss of sleep consists in the negation of, rather than union with, the other. Third, sleep is a state of rest, a state in which both desire and activity are suspended. For these reasons sleep points to the richness, i.e., to the value, freedom and reality, which lies within the individual. And this, of course, is the whole point behind the interioristic hierarchy presented in the Māṇḍūkya Upaniṣad. For the Advaitin, then, deep sleep represents the greatest degree of unification of the subject possible in phenomenal experience. For this reason the third state of consciousness serves the Advaitin as the ideal analogy for harmonious and blissful spiritual experience.[8]

(5) A fifth approach focuses on the question of the survival of personal identity during sleep. The issue is important both in itself and because of its parallel to mystical experience. The importance of the issue can be recognized through the following parallel: our entering sleep — an ocean of "unconsciousness" — and emerging from it as the same stream of consciousness which entered it, is like a river entering an ocean and re-emerging on the other side of the ocean as the same river. The parallel to mystical experience is obvious — in that at the height or in the depth of the experience the mystic ceases to exist individually and yet recovers his or her individuality on emerging from it.

But what if the mystic does not emerge from his cosmic absorption, like a person dying in sleep. "Do we say that a river after its discharge into the ocean has become an ocean-like river?"[9] P. Sankaranarayanan interprets *pratyabijñāyate,* in the sixth verse of the *Śrī Daksiṇāmūrtistotra* along these lines:

---

8. *Ibid.*, p. 104.

9. *Talks with Śrī Ramaṇa Maharṣi*, p. 173.

> But the important point in the *śloka* is the fact of *pratyabhijñā*, the linking together of the deep sleep state with the states anterior and posterior to it. This is done by the exclamation: "I slept happily, I did not know anything." This speaks of the lapse of external knowledge during sleep. But how can a person say on waking from sleep that, during sleep, he did not know anything. On waking, he can speak of his experience of that state. Whatever happened or did not happen in sleep does not continue on waking. If it did, the person cannot be said to have woken up. How then does the man who has woken from sleep say that during sleep he did not know anything? This is because, says Śrī Śaṅkara, there is an abiding identity of personality running through the sleep condition and the states prior and posterior to it. It is in virtue of that that the man who has woken from sleep (a) realises that he is the same who previously went to sleep, slept and is now awake, (b) that he did not know anything during sleep, and (c) that he slept happily. This cognition of personal identity is *pratiyabhijñā*.[10]

All these approaches indicate how crucial the comparison of the states of deep sleep and *samādhi* is for Advaita. While traditional Advaita insists that in deep sleep in "its absence of knowledge" the *jīva* "confronts but never breaks through ignorance," Ramaṇa Maharṣi offers a more daring interpretation: "deep sleep is nothing but the experience of pure *being*."[11] Consider, for instance, the following exchange:

> V.: I am asked to find out the source of "I" and in fact that is what I want to find out, but how can I? What is the source from which I came?
>
> B.: You came from the same source in which you were during sleep. Only during sleep you could not know where you

---

10. P. Sankaranarayanan, *op. cit.*, p. 231.

11. *Talks with Śrī Ramaṇa Maharṣi*, p. 173.

entered. That is why you must make the enquiry while awake.[12]

Ramaṇa would seem to be in full agreement with this account of Śaṅkara's interpretation of deep sleep that "the absence of duality in sleep reveals the non-dual nature of Absolute Consciousness itself."[13]

A similar statement is found in *Tripurā-Rahasya*:

> The concentration is possible that in deep sleep and *Samādhi*, the Self remains unqualified and therefore is not identical with the limited consciousness of the ego, "I" which is of two kinds — qualified and unqualified. Qualification implies limitations whereas its absence implies its unlimited nature.
>
> "I" is associated with limitations in dream and wakeful states, and it is free from them in deep slumber and *samādhi* states.
>
> In that case, is the "I" in *samādhi* or sleep associated with trifold division of subject, object and their relation? No! Being pure and single, it is unblemished and persists as "I-I", and nothing else. The same is Perfection.[14]

According to Ramaṇa, when we wake up and the mind begins to function it cannot bring the experience within any of its categories and therefore regards it as a form of "unconsciousness" and marginalizes it, just as if we hear a

---

12. Arthur Osborne, ed., *The Teachings of Bhagavān Śrī Ramaṇa Maharṣi in His Own Words*, Tiruvannamalai: Sri Ramanasramam, 1971, p. 56. Ramaṇa's position here seems to go beyond even that of Sarvajñātman, according to whom, in deep sleep, "the pure self as bliss is directly perceived by *Jīva*s through some subtle functioning of *Avidyā*" (Dinesh Chandra Bhattacharya, *op. cit.*, p. 261).
13. William Indich, *op. cit.*, p. 97.
14. Swami Sri Ramanananda Saraswathi, tr., *op. cit.*, p. 122.

language we cannot understand we dismiss it as gibberish. But because the state of sleep is not one of *manonāśa*, or destruction of the mind, but more like *manolaya*, or cessation of mental activity, pure being is not realized: "In a cloudy dark night no individual identification of objects is possible and there is only dense darkness, *although the seer has his eyes wide open*; similarly in *suṣupti* the seer is aware of simple nescience."[15]

Ramaṇa was asked in the course of his constant references to the experience of deep sleep in the context of Self-Realization: "Do you mean to say that sleep is Self-Realization?"[16] The same question was raised several centuries ago in a less leading manner in the *Tripurā-Rahasya* and was clarified with the help of the metaphor of reflection:

> After Janaka had spoken thus, Aṣṭāvakra continued to ask:
>
> 53-54. O King, if it is as you say that the mind made passive by elimination of thoughts is quite pure and capable of manifesting Supreme Consciousness, then sleep will do it by itself, since it satisfies your condition and there is not need for any kind of effort.
>
> 55. Thus questioned by the Brāhmaṇa youth, the King replied, I will satisfy you on this point. Listen carefully.
>
> 56-63 The mind is truly abstracted in sleep. But then its light is screened by darkness, so how can it manifest its true nature? A mirror covered with tar does not reflect images but can it

---

15. *Ibid.*, p. 246. Also see page 451: "When I ask where the Self remains in one's sleep they seem to think that it is within the body, but unaware of the body and its surroundings like a man confined in a dark room. To such people it is necessary to say that the seat of Realisation is somewhere within the body."

16. *Ibid.*, p. 237.

reflect space either? Is it enough, in that case, that images are eliminated in order to reveal the space reflected in the mirror? In the same manner, the mind is veiled by the darkness of sleep and rendered unfit for illuminating thoughts. Would such eclipse of the mind reveal the glimmer of consciousness?

Would a chip of wood held in front of a single object to the exclusion of all others reflect the object simply because all others are excluded? Reflection can only be on a reflecting surface and not on all surfaces. Similarly also, realisation of the Self can only be with an alert mind and not with a stupefied one. New-born babies have no realisation of the Self for want of alertness.

Moreover pursue the analogy of a tarred mirror. The tar may prevent the images from being seen, but the quality of the mirror is not affected, for the outer coating of tar must be reflected in the interior of the mirror. So also the mind, though diverted from dreams and wakefulness, is still in the grip of dark sleep and not free from qualities. This is evident by the recollection of the dark ignorance of sleep when one wakes.[17]

---

17. Swami Sri Ramanananda Saraswathi, tr., *op. cit.*, pp. 124-25. The text contains the following intriguing statements (p. 128):

78. "All these three states, namely, *samādhi*, sleep and the instant of cognition of objects, are characterised by absence of perturbation."

79. "Their difference lies in the later recapitulation of the respective states which illumine different perceptions."

80. "Absolute Reality is manifest in *samādhi*; a void or unmanifest condition distinguishes sleep and diversity is the characteristic of cognition in wakefulness."

7

Epistemological Issues

THE metaphor of reflection is a God-send in the context of Advaitic soteriology. It is axiomatic in Advaita that the mind must be transcended if Realization is to be achieved. This naturally leads to the question: "What particular steps will be helpful to mind control?"[1] In his answer Ramaṇa draws on a whole range of metaphors of reflection towards the end of the passage.

> A. That depends on circumstances of each. *Bhakti, karma, jñāna* and *yoga* are all one. You cannot love God, without knowing him nor know without loving him. Love manifests in everything you do and that is *karma*. The adoption of mental perception (*yoga*) is the necessary preliminary before you can know or love God in the proper way.
>
> The *jñānī*s point out that the *yogī* assumes the existence of the body, its separateness from the Self and therefore advises effort for the reunion by practice of *Yoga*. The body is in the mind which has the brain for its seat which again functions by the light borrowed from another source, as admitted by the *yogī*s themselves in their fountain theory. The *jñānī* further argues if the light is borrowed it must come from its native source. Go to the source direct and do not depend on borrowed resources. Just as an iron ball comes into being as separate from the mass

1. Paul Brunton and Mudagala Venkataramiah, *Conscious Immortality*, Tiruvannamalai: Sri Ramanasramam, 1984, p. 199.

> of iron along with fiery heat, it cools down later giving up the fire, but must be again made fiery to reunite with the mass, so also, the cause of separation must also form the factor of union. Again if there is an image reflected, there must be a source and also accessories like the sun, a pot and water, for reflection. To undo the reflection, either the surface may be covered corresponding to us reaching the fountain according to the *Yogis*; or the water may be drained away which is called *tapas* i.e. the thoughts or the brain activities are made to cease: this is *jñāna-mārga*. All these are however on the assumption that the *jīva* is separate from Self or *Brahman*. But are we separate? "No" says the *jñānī*. The ego is simply wrong identity of the Self with the non-self as in the case of a colourless crystal and its background. The crystal though colourless appears red because of its background. If the background is removed, the crystal shines in its original purity. So it is with the Self and the *antaḥkaraṇas*.[2]

Ramaṇa Maharṣi emphasized that elimination or expulsion of thoughts as the direct method, as a way of realizing one's true Self particularly in the context of *jñāna-mārga*. In this context he defined the method with epigrammatic precision:

> The gap between two thoughts is our true state. It is the real self.[3]

The metaphor of reflection has been used to explain how exactly this gap could be identified to facilitate Realization:

> 33. The other perceptions require the two conditions, namely, elimination of others and concentration on the one. But Self-Realisation differs from them in that it requires only one condition: elimination of all perceptions.

---

2. *Ibid.*, pp. 199-200, emphasis added.
3. *Ibid.*, p. 169.

34. I shall tell you the reason for this. Although consciousness is unknowable, it is still realisable by pure mind.

35-45. Even the learned are perplexed on this point. External perceptions of the mind are dependent on two conditions.

The first is elimination of other perceptions and the second is fixation on the particular item of perception. If the mind is simply turned away from other perceptions, the mind is in an indifferent state, where there is absence of any kind of perception. Therefore concentration on a particular item is necessary for the perception of external things. But since consciousness is the Self and not apart from the mind, concentration on it is not necessary for its realisation. It is enough that other perceptions (namely, thoughts) should be eliminated from the mind and then the Self will be realised.

If a man wants to pick out one particular image among a series of images passing in front of him as reflections on a mirror, he must turn his attention away from the rest of the pictures and fix it on that particular one.

If on the other hand, he wants to see the space reflected it is enough that he turns away his attention from the pictures and the space manifests without any attention on his part, for, space is immanent everywhere and is already reflected there. However it has remained unnoticed because the interspatial images dominated the scene.

Space being the supporter of all and immanent in all, becomes manifest if only the attention is diverted from the panorama. In the same way, consciousness is the supporter of all and is immanent in all and always remains perfect like space pervading the mind also. Diversion of attention from other items is all that is necessary for Self-Realisation. Or do you say that the Self-illuminant can ever be absent from any nook or corner?

> 46. There can indeed be no moment or spot from which consciousness is absent. Its absence means their absence also. Therefore consciousness of the Self becomes manifest by mere diversion of attention from things or thoughts.[4]

Another way of approaching the question of Realization would be to say that it is one's individuality which comes in the way of Realization. This way of putting the matter may be somewhat threatening to the reader but is in accordance with the tenets of Advaita. Ramaṇa uses the words ego, mind and individuality synonymously[5] and says in effect that individuality may be defined as the sum-total of the factors blocking Self-Realization, such Realization being our natural state![6] The problems which arise when Advaitic soteriology is framed in this manner are often answered with the help of the metaphor of reflection. The following passage from the *Advaita-Bodha-Dīpikā* serves to illustrate the point:

> . . . the *jīva* is changing and falsely presented on the pure Being, *Brahman*, which is the Reality. When a false thing has lost its falsity, the whole entity is gone; how can it become the Reality?
>
> 21. M.: Your doubt, how a superimposed falsity turns out to be its substratum, the Reality, is easily cleared. See how the nacre-silver ceases to be silver and remains as nacre, or a rope-snake ceasing to be snake remains over as rope. Similarly, with the *jīva* superimposed on the Reality, *Brahman*.
>
> D.: These are illusions which are not conditioned (*nirupadhika bhrama*) whereas the appearance of the *jīva* is conditioned

4. Swami Sri Ramanananda Saraswathi, tr., *Advaita Bodha Deepīkā or The Lamp of Non-dual Knowledge*, Tiruvannamalai: Sri Ramanasramam, 1967, p. 99.
5. *Talks with Śrī Ramaṇa Maharṣi*, p. 396.
6. *Ibid.*, p. 611.

> (*sopadhika bhrama*) and appears as a superimposition only on the internal faculty, the mind. So long as there is the mind, there will also be the *jīva* or the individual, and the mind is the result of past *karma*. As long as this remains unexhausted, the *jīva* must also be present. Just as the reflection of one's face is contingent upon the mirror or water in front, so is individuality, on the mind, the effect of one's past *karma*. How can this individuality be done away with?
>
> M.: Undoubtedly individuality lasts as long as the mind exists. Just as the reflected image disappears with the removal of the mirror in front, so also individuality can be effaced by stilling the mind by meditation.[7]

The next exchange is an interesting illustration of how this metaphor has run out of steam and the Guru is forced to switch metaphors.

> D.: The individuality being thus lost, the *jīva* becomes void. Having become void, how can he become *Brahman*?
>
> M.: The *jīva* is only a false appearance not apart from its substratum. It is conditional on ignorance, or the mind, on whose removal the *jīva* is left as the substratum as in the case of a dream-person.[8]

Ramaṇa, however, like some other Advaitins, maintains that nothing is more patent than one's Self. For him "there is no greater mystery than this — that being the reality we seem to gain reality. We think that there is something hiding our reality and that it must be destroyed before the reality is gained. It is ridiculous. A day will dawn when you will yourself laugh at your past efforts. That which will be on the day you laugh is also here and now."[9]

---

7. Sri Ramanananda Saraswathi, tr., *op. cit.*, p. 99.
8. *Ibid.*, p. 100.
9. David Godman, ed., *op. cit.*, p. 55.

It is in this context that Ramaṇa employs the metaphor of reflection very explicitly:

> See how each one admits that he is. Does he look into a mirror to know his being? His awareness makes him admit his existence or being. But he confuses it with the body, etc. Why should he do so? Is he aware of his body in his sleep? No; yet he himself does not cease to be in his sleep. He exists there though without the body. How does he know that he exists in sleep? Does he require a mirror to reveal his own being now? Only be aware, and your being is clear in your awareness.[10]

10. *Talks with Śrī Ramaṇa Maharṣi*, p. 332.

8

Limitations of the Metaphor

THE reflection metaphor raises a crucial issue of epistemology. What is the exact nature of the relationship between the prototype and the objects reflected in the mirror, or mirrors, or any other reflecting unit?

One way in which the relationship came to be characterized in Hindu thought was that the reflected objects are distinct but not separate. This was the view taken within Kashmir Śaivism as presented by Abhinavagupta. He wrote in the *Paramārthasāra*:

> As in the orb of a mirror pictures such as those of a town or village shine which are inseparable from it, and yet are distinct from one another and from it, so from the perfectly pure vision of the supreme Bhairava, this universe, though void of distinction appears distinct part from part and distinct from that vision.[1]

It is equally plausible, perhaps, to maintain that the relationship between the prototype and the reflection is such that they are neither the same nor different. They are too apart to be called same; they are too identical to be called different. Or they could be called both "same as well as

---

1. Quoted in T.M.P. Mahadevan, *Outlines of Hinduism*, Bombay (Mumbai): Chetana 1971, p. 175.

different" though this sounds and may well be contradictory. It is on account of this fear of contradiction after all that the Advaitins prefer to call *māyā* "neither real nor unreal," rather than both real and unreal.

There is yet another viewpoint worth considering, which is to admit that the relationship cannot be brought under a clearcut logical category. This concept that some things might only be comprehensible by being accepted as incomprehensible, was refined into the doctrine of *acintyabhedābheda* by the followers of Caitanya and may be summarized as follows:

> The relation between the souls and the world on the one hand, and God on the other is *acintyabhedābheda* (incomprehensible difference and non-difference). This is the relation that obtains between cause and effect, whole and part, possessor of power (*śaktimat*) and power (*śakti*). The relation is one of simultaneous difference and non-difference. This is, of course, inexplicable or incomprehensible. But that is a fact and cannot be denied. The example of fire and heat may be, in this connection, given. Heat is neither identical with fire, nor different from it. So is the relation of the world of souls and matter to God. It is impossible to think of this relation as falling under either of the categories, absolute difference and absolute non-difference (*bhinna-bhinnatvādi-vikalpaiś cintayitum aśakyaḥ*).[2]

Even if it be argued that prototype and reflection is not a tailormade illustration of this case, the point it deals with is the very heart of the matter here: the relationship between the *jīva*s and God. The concept of *acintyabhedābheda* comes tantalizingly close to that of *māyā* in Advaita. After all, it is said of *māyā* in Advaita:

---

2. *Ibid.*, p. 167

> It means the inexplicable; and as the explicable is what can be understood as the non-contradictory, *māyā* means the self-contradictory. It signifies that the world is full of contradictions. Yet we cannot dismiss it as unreal, because it is experienced. Therefore a concept is required to connote this peculiar quality of the world; and that concept, according to Śaṅkara, is *māyā*. Naturally, such a concept must be capable of comprehending within itself all the conflicting and contradictory statements of the Upaniṣads. That is why the Advaitins say that to prove that *māyā* is a self-contradictory idea is only to praise it and not to condemn it.[3]

There are, however, important differences to be taken into account. The first of these is that in the system of Caitanya the *jīva* is entitatively different from *Brahman*. Such is not the case in Advaita. Similarly, the incomprehensibility in the case of Caitanya's school arises because ontologically the existence of both the world and God along with the soul and God as well is conceded and it is this parity which generates incomprehensibility. The difference becomes clear if we take two Advaitin ideas into account, namely its "view of causality which makes the effect identical with the cause"[4] and the view that *māyā* is that "which produces the appearance of the world, but is not itself the appearance."[5] The *acintyabhedābheda* doctrine accepts the distinction between cause and effect and accepts *māyā* as the creative power of Īśvara.

The point involved in Advaita is somewhat different. It has to do with the perception of difference. One such attempt is found in Maṇḍana's *Brahmasiddhi*, wherein he finally

---

3. P.T. Raju, *op. cit.*, pp. 92-93.
4. Karl H. Potter, ed., *op. cit.*, p. 80.
5. K. Satchidananda Murty, *op. cit.*, p. 4.

reduces the argument at one point to the logical tenability of either of these two positions (1) difference alone is real and (2) nondifference alone is real. The reality of difference is then denied on the ground that "the idea of difference between A and B (say) presupposes a knowledge of these two entities; but the knowledge, since it points to them as *two*, already involved the idea of difference,"[6] just as other Advaitins consider the "idea of difference" as "self-discrepant" and dismisses it as "appearance." He concludes:

> So it is just as reasonable for us to assume that the usage of nondifference is in accordance with reality and that of difference with appearance.[7]

Moreover, he further concludes that instead of granting an independent ontological status to the many:

> It is more economical to assume one single thing that by its greatness appears as many.[8]

If we now revert to the metaphor of reflection as employed in the image of a city reflected in a mirror, it should not come as a total surprise that the same metaphor is employed in the second verse of the *Śrī Dakṣināmūrtistotra*, along with that of the dream, not to establish the ambiguity but the unreality of the world in relation to the ultimate. The argument may be paraphrased as follows:

> When a person dreams, he sees a number of worldly objects as if they are outside him. But strictly speaking, they are his residual mental tendencies appearing in the mind and therefore within the body. They appear to exist outside the

---

6. M. Hiriyanna, *The Essentials of Indian Philosophy*, p. 189.
7. Karl H. Potter, ed., *op. cit.*, p. 387.
8. *Ibid.*

> body, but really they have emanated from the mind. When the dream is over, the person wakes up, and he realises the truth that the dream objects were not real. Similarly, a town reflected in a mirror is not over there "in" the mirror by itself; its seeming substantiality is a projection of the town which is reflected. By these two examples, it is shown that there was no object as such in the dream or in the reflection "behind" the mirror.[9]
>
> Our metaphorical explorations have sensitized us to the fact that the dream metaphor is more apt as a metaphor for the unreality of the universe than the metaphor of reflection but their simultaneous use clearly indicates that such fine distinctions are out of place here. The ontological status of the universe hangs in precarious balance — and it is pronounced to be illusory.
>
> Really it is imbedded in the *ātman*. The power of *māyā* makes it appear as if the objects of the world exist in their own right outside of us. That dream objects have no inherent substantiality is realised when one wakes from the dream. The unreality of the reflection in the mirror is a matter of common knowledge for any sensible adult. Even so, the truth of the non-substantiality of the world and the ultimate truth of the unitary *ātman* are realised when there is direct intuitive perception (*sākātkāra*) of the non-dual *Brahman*.[10]

One notices here a difference between the use of the metaphor of reflection to illustrate the relationship of the universe to *Brahman* and of the *jīva* to *Brahman*. In the case of the universe the unreality of the image to the reality of the prototype is emphasized, but in relation to the *jīva* the point is that in "the case of the face in the mirror the prototype is identical with

---

9. P. Sankaranarayanan, *op. cit.*, p. 213.
10. *Ibid.*, pp. 213-14.

the reflection, and the reflected face is not different from the face."[11]

One particular use of the metaphor of reflection by Śaṅkara is rather impressive — when he uses it to demythologize a text, so to speak, and philosophizes it. This was alluded to earlier. In *Bṛhadāraṇyaka* I.4.7. for example the text is "speaking of Virāj or the cosmic Puruṣa and its creation, the universe, and it says at this point "He entered into it," that is, the universe. Śaṅkara says "He" is the Self, who has entered into all bodies "from *Hiraṇyagarbha* down to a blade of grass."[12]

The rationally troublesome part consists of the cosmic Puruṣa entering his own creation.

> This problem about the Self's entering itself, Śaṅkara eventually explains this using the analogy of reflection. Just as the sun "enters into" the water in the sense of being perceived there because of its reflection, so the Self enters into the undifferentiated universe in the sense of being perceived in the differentiated universe by the differentiated *jīvas*.[13]

In terms of the tradition this seems to be a reasonably satisfactory resolution.

However Śaṅkara seems to discard the use of the same analogy on the very grounds raised elsewhere, while making sense out of a much more mythically dense passage in the *Taittirīyopaniṣad* (Brahmavallī) where *Brahman* is said to enter all that he created through his austerities, right from ether to food.

---

11. Karl H. Potter, *op. cit.*, p. 86.
12. Karl H. Potter, ed., *op. cit.*, p. 185.
13. *Ibid.*

> First opponent: Then the entry may be in the sense of becoming reflected (*pratibimbatva*), as the sun is reflected in water.
>
> Second opponent: No, for *Brahman* is not limited and has no features. A thing like the sun, which has features and is limited, may be reflected, but the Self cannot be since It has no shape and is all-pervasive, and since there is thus no place outside the Self where the reflecting medium might be located. So there is no way in which *Brahman* can enter the world, and we must disregard the text in question.
>
> Śaṅkara: The passage has a different meaning, one appropriate to the context, which has to do with gaining knowledge of *Brahman*. The successive effects beginning with *ākāśa* and ending with food have been introduced in order to induce knowledge of *Brahman*; and the progress goes on through the "selves" made of breath (*prāṇa*), knowledge (*vijñāna*), and bliss (*ānanda*). When the text here speaks of "entering," it has in mind this progression, that is, that the inquisitive self — which is *Brahman* itself — enters into its own creation to rediscover itself successively. But all of this way of speaking is empirical (*vyāvahārika*), not from the highest standpoint (*pāramārthika*).[14]

It is interesting that Śaṅkara is prepared to use the metaphor when the etiology of plurality of *jīva*s is involved but is not prepared to use it when no such plurality is involved, although soteriology is. However, when the *plurality* of *jīva*s in a soteriological context is involved, he would again be prepared to use the metaphor! The following gloss on *Brahma-Sūtra* II.3.50 clearly points in that direction:

> And it is to be understood that this individual soul is a reflection of the supreme Self like the semblance of the sun in water. Not that the soul is the Self Itself, nor is it something

14. *Ibid.*, pp. 214-15.

> else. From this also it follows that just as when any one of the reflections of the sun moves, the others do not, similarly when any one individual soul becomes associated with the result of its work, no other soul is associated with it. Thus the works and the results of works do not certainly get intermixed. And since a false appearance is a creation of ignorance, it is but logical that the transmigratory state centring round that appearance must also be a creation of ignorance; and hence the instruction is logically proper that the identity of the soul with *Brahman*, which is the supreme reality, is attained by eradicating that appearance.[15]

This is how one could maintain that an individual *jīva* could be liberated consistently with other *jīva*s remaining bound, just as if one waterfilled jar in which the sun is reflected is destroyed, that image of the sun in the jar (the *jīva*) is destroyed but not the images in the other jars.[16] Others have suggested a slightly different resolution: that *māyā* is one, that "It pervades all individuals (*jīva*s) after a single individual's ignorance is destroyed through realization, just as a universal (*jāti*., e.g., cowhood) pervades all the existent individuals and is not affected by any change in their number."[17] This argument could have been used by Śaṅkara because he does not distinguish between *māyā* and *avidyā*.[18]

---

15. Swami Gambhirananda, tr., *Brahma-Sūtra-Bhāṣya of Śrī Śaṅkarācārya*, Calcutta (Kolkata): Advaita Ashrama, 1977, pp. 515-16. Note that a plurality of *avidyās* is not mentioned. This important passage has also been cited earlier.
16. Karl H. Potter, ed., *op. cit.*, p. 109.
17. Dinesh Chandra Bhattacharya, *op. cit.*, p. 261.
18. T.M.P. Mahadevan, *Superimposition in Advaita Vedānta*, pp. 18-20. Several views were developed later on. This issue is enough to introduce a note of resignation if not despair in P.T. Raju as he recounts them. "The question whether *māyā* is one or many is →

One is not entirely sure if Śaṅkara would have used this argument himself, as his concept of identity was entitative and not aggregative in character, a distinction which emerges clearly in the following remarks of Maṇḍana Miśra in the *Brahmasiddhi*:

> We see that non-difference is the basis of difference, as a face is the basis of its various reflections. The reflections are not real new different things, because their dimensions differ from the original and from each other (and therefore they are sort of error).
>
> The cognition of oneness in a collection, such as a forest of trees, is not *ultimately* based on difference, because then there would be an infinite regress, and nothing would ever be one. Whenever we do stop, that cognition will be of unity, not of difference, and therefore it will not have difference as its basis.
>
> II.29, including verses 30-31. Difference, for example, that of reflections, always appears as penetrated by the non-difference, for example, of the original object. Therefore difference is false. Similarly, the difference of the universe (*viśva*) is penetrated by the non-difference expressed by "this," "that," "object,"

→ also raised. Some say that, as it is inexplicable, that is, not logical, it may be regarded as one or many indifferently. For instance, Mādhavācārya in his *Sarvadarśanasaṁgraha*, while criticising the Sāṅkhya conception of Prakṛti, which, as one, involves the liberation of all *jīva*s when one *jīva* is liberated on Prakṛti's ceasing to be active, says that this difficulty does not arise in the Advaita as *māyā* can be both one and many. Some say that *māyā* is one and is the *upādhi* or adjunct of Īśvara, while the *avidyā*s are many and are the *upādhi*s or adjuncts of the *jīva*s. Some hold that, as the *avidyā*s are many, when one *jīva* is liberated on the destruction of one *avidyā*, the other *avidyā*s keep the other *jīva*s in bondage. These views only show the fruitlessness of attempting to bring into the moulds of logic what is admittedly illogical." (*op. cit.*, p. 116).

> "thing." In the case of differences such as that of the trees in a forest, even if we were to grant the difference in that, the unity expressed by such word as "forest" is not in each tree severally.[19]

The individual consciousness of the *jīva* is explained by Śaṅkara on the image of reflection repeatedly in the *Upadeśasāhaśrī*. It is on this analogy that Śaṅkara explains (1) the individuality or individual consciousness of the *jīva*, (2) the plurality of the *jīvas* and (3) the preparation for liberation by the *jīva*. The proof texts are as follows:

> II.17.35. Just as the reflection and the heat of the sun, perceived in water, do not belong there, so consciousness is experienced in the *buddhi* though it is not a property of the *buddhi*, since its nature is opposed to the *buddhi*.
>
> II.17.27. That seed, called *māyā*, evolves into the three states that succeed each other over and over. The Self, the locus of *māyā*, though without change and single, appears as many like reflections in the water.[20]
>
> II.17.22. When the *citta* is pure like a (clean) mirror, knowledge (*vidyā*) is revealed. So, one should take care to purify it by forbearance (*yama*), performance of the regular duties (*nityakarma*), sacrifices (*yajña*) and austerities (*tapas*).[21]

Verse II.17.27 deserves further examination as it attributes two pluralities to the operation of *māyā*. The first is the three states of being — the *avasthātraya* represented by waking, dreaming and deep sleep of the same *jīva*; the other the emergence of the pluralities of the *jīva*! From this point of view, it is interesting that the process of *saṁsāra* in some later

---

19. Karl H. Potter, ed., *op. cit.*, p. 386.
20. Karl H. Potter, ed., *op. cit.*, p. 241.
21. *Ibid.*, p. 240.

Advaitic works is not defined merely in terms of the involvement of the *jīvas* in the process of birth and rebirth; or the involvement of the *jīva* in the process of birth and rebirth but the involvement of the *jīva* in the daily round of undergoing the three states:

> 105. The *jīva* revolves in this merry-go-round owing to the operation of his past *karma* according as it bestows waking, dream or deep sleep experience. This is *saṁsāra*. In the same way the *jīva* is subject to births and deaths as a result of past karma.
>
> 106. Nevertheless they are merely appearances of the deluded mind and not real. He seems to be born and to die.
>
> D.: How can birth and death be illusory?
>
> M.: Listen carefully to what I say.
>
> 107-109. Just as when *jīva* is overcome by sleep, the bearings of the waking state give place to new ones of dream in order to reproduce past experiences, or there is total loss of all external things and mental activities, so also when he is overpowered by coma before death, the present bearings are lost and the mind lies dormant. This is death. When the mind resumes the reproduction of past experiences in new settings, the phenomenon is called birth.[22]

And there are many *jīva*s because there is one *jīva*, as intersubjectivity is mutually dependent from beginningless time.

---

22. Sri Ramanananda Saraswathi, tr., *op. cit.*, p. 18. Also see Andrew O. Fort, *The Self and Its States: A States of Consciousness Doctrine in Advaita Vedānta*, Delhi: Motilal Banarsidass, 1990.

9

Conclusion

THE metaphor of reflection, for all its richness, is also subject to certain limitations which were occasionally hinted at during the course of its exploration in the realm of Asian, Indian, Hindu and then particularly Advaitic thought. One serious limitation of the metaphor is that it can often illustrate two opposing philosophical positions with equal plausibility. Consider, for instance, the question of the *ātman*, whose relationship to the *jīva* is a central concern of Advaita. In this context Padmapāda suggests that the facial reflection is in some ways perhaps the best metaphorical representation of the relationship of identity between *jīva* and *Brahman*. The passage from the *Pañcapādikā* is presented in extenso below as it helps to identify several limitations of the metaphor, some of which are identified in the passage itself:

> Question: Why are they identical?
>
> Answer: For example, Devadatta has certain features when outside the house, and he is also recognized to have those same features when he goes inside. This recognition would not be possible if the "two Devadattas" were different; no more would it be possible to recognize Devadatta's reflection in the mirror if it were not identical with him — in that case we should have to say that the mirror transforms itself when the prototype (*bimba*) is nearby. Nor does the prototype leave its impression as does a seal, since the reflection is not (necessarily)

the same size as the prototype, since there is no contact between the prototype and the mirror, and since if it were thus the mirror would continue to reflect the prototype even after it was removed.

Question: Perhaps the mirror is like the rolled-up mat that, having been spread out by some circumstance, rolls back up again as soon as the circumstance disappears.

Answer: The cause of the mat rolling up is the dispositional tendency (*saṁskāra*) it has gotten because of being rolled up for a long time, not the removal of any circumstance. So a mirror that had been in the vicinity of a certain object for a long time ought, by analogy, to remain with a tendency to reflect that object even when the object has disappeared — but we know that doesn't happen.

Opponent: Very well — the reflection is not a different object from its prototype; still, it is not really identical with the prototype, any more than the silver falsely found in a shell is really identical with real silver.

Answer: The cases are not the same, for in the shell-silver case the silver is sublated, whereas in the mirror-reflection case the reflection (though it disappears) is not sublated (i.e., we do not judge "this reflection is not my face").

Opponent: Well, doesn't "that art thou" sublate error?

Answer: No, what it says is that the *jīva* (= reflection or *pratibimba*) has the same nature as *Brahman* (= prototype or *bimba*). If it were sublatory it would be negative — "thou are not" analogous to "(this is) not silver."

Prābhākara: How can one thing that manifests itself completely in two separate places really be in both?

Answer: We don't say that a single thing can really manifest itself completely in separate places at the same time, but we do say that such a thing is single. Its appearance as many is due to *māyā*, which is good at producing impossible appearances.

Objection: Even when we apprehend the identity of the reflection with its prototype they still appear to be separate; likewise, even when we apprehend the identity of the *jīva* with *Brahman* their separateness still continues to be manifested; thus it cannot be got rid of.

Answer: Though Devadatta's knowledge that the reflection in the mirror is identical with his face cannot destroy the mirror — which is why the separation continues to appear — the *jīva*'s knowledge sublating the difference between *jīva* and *Brahman* destroys all the adjuncts including the internal organ (*antaḥkaraṇa*) that is the reflecting medium.

Objection: Both the mirror image and the rose-coloured crystal arise because there is a real object nearby — the mirror or the rose — whereas in the case of the supposedly false appearance of the *jīva* there is no such real object to serve as adjunct.

Answer: That's why scripture alludes to the case of the rope-snake.

Opponent: Even in the rope-snake case, though the snake is not there, the trace of some past experience of snake must be, and it acts as the adjunct.

Answer: Yes, and the difference is that in all three cases — mirror image, rosy crystal and rope-snake — traces must operate, but in the first two some other object is present whereas in the last one there is no such entity. Still, from these three examples it is not made clear that the "prototype" — the face, the flower or the rope — may be unrelated to other elements in the situation. This point, however, is brought out in still another familiar analogy from scripture, that is, the example of the *ākāśa* in a pot, for there the "prototype" — the *ākāśa* — is unrelated to the pot, the adjunct.

Not that these examples are sufficient in themselves to prove the point; they merely assist the *pramāṇa*s by removing doubts

> that may arise. And so we conclude that the Self is "not this" but is figuratively spoken of as "this" in practical affairs."[1]

In Advaita, liberation dawns with the realization of the *ātman*; in Buddhism it dawns with the realization that there is no *ātman*. The metaphor of reflection has presumably been employed in the case of Padmapāda to facilitate the realization of *ātman* but in the case of *ānanda*, the cousin and favoured disciple of Buddha, the realization that there is no *ātman* is said to have dawned through a similar metaphorical realization, as there is nothing underlying the image.

Even within the framework of Advaita, however, the metaphor of reflection needs to be examined more closely. The assumption here is that the object and the reflection of the object are identical. This is all right if one wishes to connect *ātman* with *Brahman*. But in that case *ātman* is *Brahman* and to say the one is a reflection of the other is to misrepresent the Advaitic position. In this case the point is understated — for the identity of *ātman* and *Brahman* is of a kind which does not even allow for a prior separation, albeit by reflection. But the metaphor connects the *jīva* with *Brahman*. It is true that Advaitic literature speaks of this likeness, and the account of the two birds in the *Muṇḍakopaniṣad* is perhaps as good an illustration of this point as any (III.I. 1-2):

> 1. Two birds, companions (who are) always united, cling to the self-same tree. Of these two, the one eats the sweet fruit and the other looks on without eating.
>
> 2. On the self-same tree, a person immersed (in the sorrows of the world) is deluded and grieves on account of his helplessness. When he sees the other, the Lord who is

1. Karl H. Potter, ed., *op. cit.*, pp. 575-76.

> worshipped and his greatness, he becomes freed from sorrow.[2]

But the whole point of Advaita seems to be that while on the one hand the *jīva* is so like the *Brahman,* in fact is *Brahman,* on the other hand the *jīva* is so unlike *Brahman,* in the saṁsāric condition. In that case would not the introduction of a distorted surface enrich the metaphor. In other words, while caught up in the process of *saṁsāra,* we are looking at ourselves through concave and convex mirrors as it were and take ourselves to be looking the way we don't look; and liberation then would be like looking at ourselves in a mirror with an even surface (which invests the virtue of equanimity with a new significance.) The same point is sometimes made in another way: by comparing our reflections in a dirty and clear mirror and taking ourselves to be dirty when we are not. The problem here is that the *jīva* is Janus-faced: when looking at *Brahman,* it is **sameness** which calls for recognition; when looking at the world the **difference** demands attention.

At this point the question of the reflecting medium must now be brought into the picture. As Karl H. Potter notes:

> An implication of Padmapāda's analysis is that when one appreciates the identity of *jīva* and *Brahman* it does not follow that the medium — the internal organ — is destroyed, any more than it is the case when one realizes that one's face is destroyed. This is handy, *for it explains why upon liberation the jīva does not immediately disappear.* When pressed about this with the objection that his model requires a distinct, separate medium, Padmapāda immediately has recourse to the rope-snake analogy, or, alternatively, the pot-space analogy. In both the latter cases, the prototype (analogous to *Brahman*) is not

---

2. S. Radhakrishnan, ed., *The Principal Upaniṣads,* London: George Allen & Unwin, 1953, p. 686.

> related to the rest of the items in the model (analogous to the adjuncts, including the medium).[3]

The contradiction is now easily resolved. In relation to the world, the medium — the mind, is a help and helps explain why upon liberation the *jīva* does not immediately disappear. But in relation to *Brahman* the analogy fails. Although the rope-snake metaphor does have the merit here of eliminating the medium, it is not a good example because the snake is so different from the rope, whereas it is the identity or at least similarity and not difference which needs to be emphasized here. For the same reason the analogy of the flower and the red crystal does not work well here for reasons Padmapāda himself recognizes:

> (This case contrasts with that of a face reflected in a mirror.) There the point is that the face and its reflection are actually identical, so that the error comes in thinking them different (whereas in the crystal-flower case the redness of the crystal is similar to but not identical with the redness of the flower). So by analogy in "I am not, as in the ego sense case, merely the apparent sharer of consciousness with *Brahman*.[4]

The pot-space metaphor seems to work best of all, a point again recognized by Padmapāda as noted earlier:

> Answer: Yes, and the difference is that in all three cases — mirror image, rosy crystal and rope-snake — traces must operate, but in the first two some other object is present whereas in the last one there is no such entity. Still, from these three examples it is not made clear that the "prototype" — the face, the flower or the rope — may be unrelated to other elements in the situation. This point, however, is brought out in still another

3. Karl H. Potter, ed., *op. cit.*, p. 86, emphasis added. This passage was also cited earlier.

4. *Ibid.*, pp. 574-75.

> familiar analogy from scripture, that is, the example of the *ākāśa* in a pot, for there the "prototype" — the *ākāśa* — is unrelated to the pot, the adjunct.[5]

This brings us again to a consideration of some other limitations of the metaphor. It is true that once the medium is in place, the rest of the process becomes less problematical:

> It is the apparent production of individual selves that most requires explanation, for the materials with which to develop the explanation are sparse. Once we assume that somehow attributeless *Brahman* has been veiled (by itself? by *avidyā*, anyhow) and become apparently diversified into many *jīva*s, along with an omniscient, omnipotent God, the rest of the story becomes much easier to tell. With internal organs to function as reflecting media, projection of a variety of objects for the *jīva*s to cognize is understandable along lines sketched above.[6]

But there are problems and Karl H. Potter seems to hint at them in his discussion of Śaṅkara:

> Just what does constitute the reflecting medium is not clearly answerable on the basis of Śaṅkara's writings. We have seen so far that undifferentiated Prakṛti of the internal organ (*buddhi*) can be cast in the role. In other places other items are so cast — *prajñā, prāṇa,* and *citta* among them. But of course, it is Śaṅkara's view that ultimately there is no medium distinct from *Brahman* Itself. This would seem to suggest that the first projection cannot be understood on the reflection model, though later ones can, and Śaṅkara's discussion in one or two places seems to endorse that idea. The original projection is more like dreaming, or a magic show.[7]

---

5. *Ibid.*, p. 576. This passage was also cited earlier.
6. *Ibid.*, p. 87.
7. *Ibid.*, p. 85.

One way in which later Advaita tried to resolve this issue was by distinguishing between *māyā* and *avidyā*[8] or by speculating on the exact nature of the relationship between *Brahman* and *māyā*. But T.M.P. Mahadevan insists that in Śaṅkara, *māyā* and *avidyā* are synonymous.[9] It also seems to be the case that, for Śaṅkara, relationship of *Brahman* and *māyā* contains an elusive element of *anirvacanīyatā*.

The metaphor of reflection is used in relation to consciousness and this brings up another limitation. A limitation of the metaphor of reflection in relation to consciousness at any stage consists of the fact that the reflecting surface, say, a mirror, is insentient (unless one is seeing a reflection in someone's eye!). This limitation is twofold — not only does it make the image lack consciousness, it also obscures the fact that images and live images at that, can emerge from consciousness. This seems to be the import of the following passage from *Tripurā-Rahasya*:

> Those qualities of reflected images depend on the excellence of the reflecting surface, we can see in the case of water and polished surface. Mirrors are insentient and are not self-contained. Whereas, consciousness is always pure and self-contained; it does not require an external object to create the image. Ordinary mirrors are liable to be soiled by extraneous dirt whereas consciousness has nothing foreign to it, being always alone and undivided; and therefore its reflections are unique. Created things are not self-luminous and are illuminated by another's cognitive faculty. Cognition of things implies their images on our intelligence. They are only images. The creation therefore is an image. It is not self-shining; and thus it is not self-aware, but becomes a fact on our perception

8. Dinesh Chandra Bhattacharya, *op. cit.*, p. 267, etc.
9. T.M.P. Mahadevan, *Superimposition in Advaita Vedānta*, pp. 32-36.

of it. Therefore I say that the universe is nothing but an image on our consciousness. Consciousness shines notwithstanding the formation of images on it; though impalpable, it is steadily fixed and does not falter. Just as the images in a mirror are not apart from the mirror, so also the creations of consciousness are not apart from it.

64. Objects are necessary for producing images in a mirror; they are not however necessary for consciousness because it is self-contained.

65-66 . . . O Paraśurāma! Note how day-dreams and hallucinations are clearly pictured in the mind even in the absence of any reality behind them. How does it happen? The place of objects is taken up by the peculiar imaginative quality of the mind. When such imagination is deep, it takes shape as creation; consciousness is pure and unblemished in the absence of imagination.

67. Thus you see how consciousness was absolute and pure before creation and how its peculiar quality or will brought about this image of the world in it.[10]

The superiority of the metaphor of the "mental images" as distinguished from "reflected images" in this context are clearly spelled out by Ramaṇa Maharṣi:

Further on, Sri Bhagavan Ramaṇa continued:

The mirror reflects objects; yet they are not real because they cannot remain apart from the mirror. Similarly, the world is said to be a reflection in the mind as it does not remain in the absence of mind. The question arises: if the universe is a reflection, there must be a real object known as the universe in order that it might be reflected in the mind. This amounts to an admission of the existence of an objective universe. Truly speaking, it is not so.

---

10. Swami Sri Ramanananda Saraswathi, tr., pp. 84-85.

> Therefore the *dream* illustration is set forth. The dream world has no objective existence. How then is it created? Some mental impressions should be admitted. They are called *vāsanās*. How were the *vāsanās* in the mind? the answer is: they were subtle. Just as a whole tree is contained potentially in a seed, so the world is in the mind.[11]

The same measure had to be adopted in the *Upadeśasāhaśrī* in the face of a similar objection:

> Objection: In order to know that something is a reflection of the Self we must know that the Self exists independently of the reflection. But in order to know that the Self exists independently of the reflection we must know that the thing is a reflection of the Self. So your case depends on mutual dependence (*anyonyāśraya*).
>
> Answer: No, for in dreams notions and the seer are known to be distinct. In that state there are no (external) chariots, etc. so that the Self must directly apprehend the ideas.[12]

The fourth limitation of the metaphor of reflection is a somewhat curious one. One of the problems in Advaita is to explain how, or in what manner, after Realization, the Realized one continues to perceive the world although its falsity has been realized. Ramaṇa Maharṣi provides what seems a helpful analogy: "For instance you see a reflection in the mirror and the mirror. You know the mirror to be the reality and the picture to be a mere reflection. Is it necessary that to see the mirror we should cease to see the reflection in it?"[13] After the initial excitement caused by the clarity and

---

11. *Talks with Śrī Ramaṇa Maharṣi*, pp. 412-13.
12. Karl H. Potter, ed., *op. cit.*, p. 248.
13. David Godman, ed., *The Teachings of Śrī Ramaṇa Maharṣi*, New York: Arkana, 1985, p. 42.

novelty wears off, one again asks: but the mirror is inert and the Realized one is alive. Ramaṇa's answer could be that the mind of the Realized one is "dead" in a manner of speaking[14] but he also concedes elsewhere that it functions as pure mind. It is here that the metaphor of reflection is again further helpful:

> D.: Will the description of *Brahman* as *sat-cit-ānanda* suit this *śuddha manas*? For this too will be destroyed in the final emancipation.
>
> M.: If *śuddha manas* is admitted, the Bliss (*ānanda*) experienced by the *Jñānī* must also be admitted to be reflected. This reflection must finally merge into the Original. Therefore the *jīvanmukti* state is compared to the reflection of a spotless mirror in another similar mirror. What will be found in such a reflection? Pure *Ākāśa* (ether). Similarly, the *Jñānī*'s reflected Bliss (*ānanda*) represents only the true Bliss.
>
> These are all only words. It is enough that a person becomes *antarmukhi* (inward-bent). The *sāstras* are not needed for an inward mind. They are meant for the rest.[15]

At this point the resources of the metaphor are well-nigh exhausted and a remark by the neo-Confucianist Shao Yung (1011-1077) becomes surprisingly relevant:

> A mirror reflects because it does not obscure the corporeal form of things. But water [with its purity] does even better because it reveals the universal character of the corporeal form of things as they really are. And the sage does still better because he reflects the universal character of the feelings of all things.

---

14. *Talks with Śrī Ramaṇa Maharṣi*, pp. 435, 244.

15. *Ibid.*, p. 498, emphasis added. For more on the status of *jīvanmukti*, see Andrew O. Fort, *Jīvanmukti in Transformatoin: Embodied Liberation in Advaita and Neo-Vedānta*, Albany, N.Y.: State University of New York Press, 1998.

> The sage can do so because he views things as things view themselves; that is, not subjectively but from the viewpoint of things. Since he is able to do this, how can there be anything between him and things?[16]

Another approach has been adopted by those who would continue to associate the sage's Realization with the metaphor of reflection. In one case, in the presence of Ramaṇa:

> The questioner quoted that the mind starved of ideas amounted to realisation and asked what the experience is in that state. He himself read out a passage from Mr. Brunton that it was describable. The answer was there. He again ventured out that it must be like looking through an unsilvered mirror, as contrasted with the present experience corresponding to looking on a silvered mirror.
>
> Sri Bhagavan said it was a mirror facing another clear mirror, i.e., no reflection.[17]

The need to remove the reflecting medium is felt both etiologically and eschatologically in Advaita. It sometimes leads to a kind of an impasse in the eschatological context:

> D.: Does Bhagavan see the world as part and parcel of Himself? How does He see the world?
>
> M.: The Self alone is and nothing else. However, it is differentiated owing to ignorance. Differentiation is threefold: (1) of the same kind; (2) of a different kind; and (3) as parts in itself. The world is not another self similar to the self. It is not different from the self; nor is it part of the self.
>
> D.: Is not the world reflected on the Self?

16. Wm. Theodore de Bary et al, eds., *op. cit.*, vol. I, p. 465.
17. *Talks with Śrī Ramaṇa Maharṣi*, p. 464, emphasis added.

M.: For reflection there must be an object and an image. But the Self does not admit of these differences.

D.: Does not then Bhagavan see the world?

M.: Whom do you mean by Bhagavan?

D.: A *jīva* advanced more than I.

M.: If you understand your *jīva* another *jīva* is also understood.[18]

It is an impasse, as it is precisely the not-so-advanced *jīva* who is trying to understand the advanced *jīva*.

However, even in the broader context of adjusting the claims of metaphysical and empirical realities, the metaphor does not fare as badly, as the following dialogue reveals:

Baron Von Veltheim-Ostran, an East German Baron asked, "There should be harmony between knowledge of the Self and knowledge of the world. They must develop side by side. Is it right? Does Maharṣi agree?"

M.: Yes.

D.: Beyond the intellect and before wisdom dawns there will be pictures of the world passing before one's consciousness. Is it so?

Sri Bhagavan pointed out the parallel passage in *Dakṣiṇāmūrti stotram* to signify that the pictures are like reflections in a mirror; again from the Upaniṣad — as in the mirror, so in the world of manes; as in the water, so in the world of *Gandharvas*; as shadow and sunlight in Brahma Loka.[19]

The metaphor also works when the process of Realization is being explained in the context of the three bodies — the *kāraṇa*, the *sūkṣma* and the *sthūla*. The question is: how does

18. *Ibid.*, p. 217.

19. *Ibid.*, p. 107.

the *jñānī*'s body function without the mind? Ramaṇa Maharṣi explains as follows:

> A *jñānī* has his *kāraṇa śarīra* destroyed; the *sthūla śarīra* (gross body) has no effect on him and is for all practical purposes destroyed too. The *sūkṣma śarīra* (subtle body) alone remains. It is otherwise called *ativāhika śarīra*. It is this which is held by all persons after the physical body is given up. And with this they traverse to their *loka*s until another suitable physical body is taken. The *jñānī* is supposed to move in *Brahmaloka* with this *sūkṣma śarīra*. Then that is also dissolved and he passes to final Liberation.
>
> The whole explanation is meant only for the onlooker. The *jñānī* himself will never raise such questions. He knows by his experience that he is not bound by any kind of limitations.
>
> D.: What is the "final emancipation" according to the foregoing explanation?
>
> M.: The *ativāhika* or the *sūkṣma śarīra* corresponds to the pure light which one experiences just after sleep and before the rise of the ego. It is Cosmic Consciousness. That is only the Light reflected from the Heart. When the reflection ceases and abides as the Original Light in the Heart it is final emancipation.

So far so good. But then a curve is thrown.

> D.: But *Yoga Vāśiṣṭha* says that the *citta* (mind) of a *jīvanmukta* is *acala* (unchanging).
>
> M.: So it is. *Acala citta* (unchanging mind) is the same as *śuddha manas* (pure mind). The *jñānī's manas* is said to be *suddha manas*. The *Yoga Vāśiṣṭha* also says that *Brahman* is no other than the *jñānī's* mind. So *Brahman* is *śuddha manas* only.
>
> D.: Will the description of *Brahman* as *sat-cit-ānanda* suit this *śuddha manas*? For this too will be destroyed in the final emancipation.

> M.: If *śuddha manas* is admitted, the Bliss (*ānanda*) experienced by the *jñānī* must also be admitted to be reflected. This reflection must finally merge into the Original. Therefore the *jīvanmukti* state is compared to the reflection of a spotless mirror in another similar mirror. What will be found in such a reflection? Pure *ākāśa* (ether). Similarly, the *jñānī*'s reflected Bliss (*ānanda*) represents only the true Bliss.
>
> These are all only words. It is enough that a person becomes *antarmukhī* (inward-bent). The *śāstra*s are not needed for an inward turned mind. They are meant for the rest.[20]

In fact a host of limitations of the metaphor of reflection can be identified in Ramaṇa Maharṣi's efforts to utilize it especially in the context to Realization. So long as it is used merely to illustrate a point, without the metaphor being pushed further, it does not present much difficulty. In the following passage, for example, the mirror is used along with the cinema show to indicate the illusory nature of the universe.

> D.: Are there degrees of illusion?
>
> M.: Illusion is itself illusory. Illusion must be seen by one beyond it. Can such a seer be subject to illusion? Can he then speak of degrees of illusion?
>
> There are scenes floating on the screen in a cinema show. Fire appears to burn buildings to ashes. Water seems to wreck vessels. But the screen on which the pictures are projected remains unscorched and dry. Why?
>
> Because the pictures are unreal and the screen is real.
>
> Again reflections pass through a mirror; but the mirror is not in any way affected by the quality or quantity of the reflections on it.

---

20. *Ibid.*, p. 498. Diacritics supplied.

> So the world is a phenomenon on the single Reality, which is not affected in any manner. Reality is only one.
>
> The discussion about illusion is due to the difference in the angle of vision. Change your angle of vision to one of *jñāna* and then find the universe to be only Brahman. Being now in the world, you see the world as such. Get beyond it and this will disappear: The Reality alone will shine.[21]

Another limitation of the metaphor pertains not to the need to postulate a reflecting medium, but rather to the question: how could pure consciousness be reflected as it possesses no sensible qualities. Two answers which have been suggested are found alongside in *Upadeśasāhaśrī* but both present difficulties:

> II.17.34. Just as Rāhu, though invisible, is seen as a reflection in the moon, so the Self, though omnipresent, is grasped in the Buddhi.[22]

The example of Rāhu is problematical because there it is the reflection itself which is called Rāhu's head, there is no Rāhu's head which is reflected. The issue is further complicated by the fact that Rāhu's head is an example of *vikalpa* or "mere verbal idea caused by words, to which no real facts correspond. When you hear the words "Rāhu's head," you have the idea of a distinction between Rāhu and its head, although really there is no distinction between the two, Rāhu being only a head."[23] And that head too is only a reflection itself! Śaṅkara is not unaware of this for he remarks

21. *Ibid.*, p. 217.
22. Karl H. Potter, ed., *op. cit.*, p. 241. See also page 246.
23. Satischandra Chatterjee and Dhirendramohan Datta, *An Introduction to Indian Philosophy*, Calcutta (Kolkata): University of Calcutta (Kolkata), 1950, p. 301.

in the *Upadeśasāhaśrī*: "If Rāhu is taken to be already proved as real, the reflection of the face is not, and the example is irrelevant. But if Rāhu is taken to be a shadow, then it is unreal as we have shown."[24] In the other verse, consciousness is compared to the sun which is an object. The same problem applies to the succeeding verse.

The limitations of the metaphor of reflection are thus obvious. Any metaphor can be pressed only up to a point, when it has to be either abandoned or switched. In fact, in some cases, while in one account some metaphors are used without any qualifications, in other accounts in more or less the same context, the expositor shows greater consciousness of the limitations. The passage which is cited below has been selected from *Talks with Śrī Ramaṇa Maharṣi*. A portion similar to this passage with an unqualified use of the crystal metaphor by Ramaṇa Maharṣi was cited earlier from *Conscious Immortality*, a record of conversations of Ramaṇa Maharṣi with Paul Brunton.[25] The extract below is distinguished by the fact that herein the use of a metaphor is immediately followed by a comment on its limitation. The reader may wish to compare the two passages. I have underscored the lines showing a new awareness of the limitations of the metaphor. Both the passages fall in the 1935-1939 period. It is clear, however, that they represent comments made on two different occasions.

> Again if there is an image reflected there must be a source and also accessories like the Sun and a pot of water for reflection. To do away with the reflection either the surface is covered up

24. Karl H. Potter, ed., *op. cit.*, p. 243.
25. Paul Brunton and Mudagala Vankatramiah, *op. cit.*, pp. 199-200. See note 107.

> corresponding to reaching the fontanelle according to the yogis or the water is drained away which is called *tapas* (*tapo brahmeti* — *tapas* is *Brahman*). That is to say, the thoughts or the brain activities are made to cease. This is *jñāna-mārga*.
>
> All these are however on the assumption that the *jīva* is separate from the Self or *Brahman*. But are we separate? "No," says the *jñānī*. The ego is simply wrong identity of the Self with the non-self, as in the case of a colourless crystal and its coloured background. If the background is removed the crystal shines in its original purity. So it is with the Self and the *antaḥkarana*s.
>
> Still again the illustration is not quite appropriate. For the ego has its source from the Self and is not separate like the background from the crystal. Having its source from the Self, the ego must only be retraced in order that it might merge in its source.[26]

But perhaps one was too quick in pointing out this limitation. For the ego is traced to its source here, just as an image can be traced to its prototype.

---

26. *Talks with Śrī Ramaṇa Maharṣi*, pp. 366-67.

Bibliography

Bhattacharya, Dinesh Chandra, 1953, "Post-Śaṅkara Advaita," in Haridas Bhattacharyya, ed., *The Cultural Heritage of India*, vol. III pp. 255-80, Calcutta (Kolkata): The Ramakrishna Mission Institute of Culture.

Brunton, Paul and Venkataramiah, Mudagala, eds., 1984, *Conscious Immortality*, Tiruvannamalai: Sri Ramanasramam.

Chatterjee, Satischandra and Datta Dhirendramohan, 1950, *An Introduction to Indian Philosophy*, Calcutta (Kolkata): University of Calcutta.

Ch'en, Kenneth K.S., 1968, *Buddhism: The Light of Asia*, Woodbury, New York: Barron's Educational Series.

———, 1964, *Buddhism in China: A Historical Survey*, Princeton, New Jersey: Princeton University Press.

Conze, Edward *et al.*, eds., 1964, *Buddhist Texts Through the Ages*, New York: Harper & Row.

de Bary, Wm. Theodore *et al.*, eds., 1960, *Sources of Chinese Tradition*, New York: Columbia University Press.

Deutsch, Eliot and Van Buitenen, J.A.B., eds., 1971, *A Source book of Advaita Vedānta*, Honolulu: The University Press of Hawaii.

———, and Dalvi, Rohit, eds., 2004, *The Essential Vedānta: A New Source Book of Advaita Vedānta*, Bloomington, Indiana: World Wisdom Inc.

Fort, Andrew O., 1998, *Jīvanmukti in Transformation: Embodied Liberation in Advaita and Neo-Vedānta*, Albany, N.Y.: State University of New York Press.

———, 1990, *The Self and Its States: A States of Consciousness Doctrine in Advaita Vedānta*, Delhi: Motilal Banarsidass.

Gambhirananda, Swami, tr., 1977, *Brahma-Sūtra-Bhāṣya of Śrī Śaṅkarācārya*, Calcutta (Kolkata): Advaita Ashrama.

Godman, David, ed., 1985, *The Teachings of Śrī Ramaṇa Maharṣi*, New York: Arkana.

Grimes, John A., 2004, *The Vivekacūdāmaṇi of Śaṅkarācārya Bhagavatpāda: An Introduction and Translation*, Hants, England: Ashgate Publishing Limited.

———, 1994, *Problems and Perspectives in Religious Discourse: Advaita Vedānta Implications*, Albany, N.Y.: State University of New York Press.

Hiriyanna, M., 1948, *The Essentials of Indian Philosophy*, London: George Allen & Unwin.

———, 1932, *Outlines of Indian Philosophy*, London: George Allen & Unwin.

Indich, William M., 1980, *Consciousness in Advaita Vedānta*, Delhi: Motilal Banarshidass.

Kanoaka, S., 1960, "Ādarśa-Jñāna," in G.P. Malalasekara, ed., *Encyclopaedia of Buddhism*, Colombo: Government of Ceylon (Sri Lanka).

Kapleau, Philip, ed., 1966, *Three Pillars of Zen*, New York: Harper & Row.

Madhavananda, Swami, tr., 1966, *Vivekacūḍāmaṇi of Śrī Śaṅkarācārya*, Calcutta (Kolkata): Advaita Ashrama.

Mahadevan, T.M.P., 1960, *Gauḍapāda: A Study in Early Advaita*, Madras (Chennai): University of Madras.

———, 1971, *Outlines of Hinduism*, Bombay (Mumbai): Chetana.

———, 1985, *Superimposition in Advaita Vedānta*, New Delhi: Sterling Publishers Private Ltd.

Mukherjee, Radhakamal, 1971, *The Song of the Supreme (Aṣṭāvakragīta)*, Delhi: Motilal Banarsidass.

Murty, K. Satchidananda, 1974, *Revelation and Reason in Advaita Vedānta*, Delhi: Motilal Banarsidass.

Potter, Karl H., ed., 1981, *Encyclopaedia of Indian Philosophies*, vol. III. Delhi: Motilal Banarsidass.

Organ, Troy Wilson, 1974, *Hinduism: Its Historical Development*, Woodbury, New York: Barron's Educational Series.

Osborne, Arthur, ed., 1971, *The Teachings of Śrī Ramaṇa Maharṣi in His Own Words*, Tiruvannamalai: Sri Ramanasramam.

Radhakrishnan, S., ed., 1953, *The Principal Upaniṣads*, London: George Allen & Unwin.

Rajneesh, Bhagwan Shree, 1972, *I Am the Gate*, Bombay (Mumbai): A Life Awakening Movement Publication.

Raju, P.T., 1952, *The Idealist Thought of India*, London: George Allen & Unwin.

Ram-Prasad, Chakravarthi, 2002, *Advaita Epistemology and Metaphysics: An Outline of Indian Non-Realism*, London: Routledge Curzon.

Ramanasramam, Sri, 1984, *Talks with Śrī Ramaṇa Maharṣi*, Tiruvannamalai.

Rambachan, Anantanand, 1991, *Accomplishing the Accomplished: The Vedas as a Source of Valid Knowledge in Advaita Vedānta*, Honolulu: University of Hawaii Press.

Rao, Srinivasa, 1985, *Advaita: Critical Investigation*, Bangalore: Indian Philosophy Foundation.

Roodurmun, P.S., 2002, *Bhāmatī and Vivaraṇa Schools of Advaita Vedānta: A Critical Approach*, Delhi: Motilal Banarsidass.

Sankaranarayanan, P., 1970, *What is Advaita?*, Bombay (Mumbai): Bharatiya Vidya Bhavan.

Saraswathi, Swami Sri Ramanananda, tr., 1967, *Advaita Bodh Deepīkā or The Lamp of Non-Dual Knowledge*, Tiruvannamalai: Sri Ramanasramam.

———, tr., 1980, *Tripura Rahasya or the Mystery Beyond the Trinity*, Tiruvannamalai: Sri Ramanasramam.

Suzuki, Daisetz T., 1959, *Zen and Japanese Culture*, New York: Pantheon Books.

Author Index

Subject Index